MIND OVER MATTER

Examines the evidence for the fascinating phenomenon
of psychokinesis.

MIND
OVER MATTER
How the human mind can manipulate the physical world

by

D. SCOTT ROGO

THE AQUARIAN PRESS

First published 1986

© D. SCOTT ROGO 1986

British Library Cataloguing in Publication Data

Rogo, D. Scott
Mind over matter.
1. Psychokinesis
I. Title
133.8'8   BF1371

ISBN 0-85030-485-7

*The Aquarian Press is part of the
Thorsons Publishing Group, Wellingborough, Northamptonshire,
NN8 2RQ, England*

Printed in Great Britain by Woolnough Bookbinding Limited, Irthlingborough,
Northamptonshire

3 5 7 9 10 8 6 4 2

Contents

Introduction

This book deals with a very unusual subject. It concerns a phenomenon in which mankind believes yet questions at the same time. This statement may sound paradoxical but it really isn't.

Do you believe that, by merely willing it, you can make a little bottle slide across a table several feet away? You probably don't. Or would you believe that through mental concentration you could make dice fall on the same side several times in a row? Again, probably not. Probably nor do most of the people with whom you interact during the course of your daily life.

On the other hand, though, have you ever prayed in the hope that somehow your silent thoughts might influence material situations? Or that of a friend's? Have you ever hit a golf ball or thrown a bowling ball and given it a little mental boost to help it along a bit if it seemed headed toward missing its mark?

Just as you would unhesitatingly respond negatively to the first group of questions, you might feel no embarrassment in answering affirmatively to the latter ones. This is the paradox about which I am speaking. On a conscious level, the idea that we can influence the material world merely by an act of mind or will is so counter to our materialistic matter-of-fact way of looking at the world that we reject it out of hand. Yet on an intuitive level we seem to realize that somehow our thoughts *can* break out of the private world of our minds.

In ancient times, philosophers would argue for days upon end over such issues as the relationship between the mind and body, the mind and the brain, the mind and the outside world, *ad infinitum.* The rise of the Renaissance, however, brought with it the wonderful idea that it was better to test a theory experimentally than merely to argue over it. It was at this time that scholars and philosophers first began to consider seriously whether or not the mind could directly influence the outside world . . . perhaps through some hidden force.

The concept that the mind can directly manipulate physical matter is not an idea that sprang from some science fiction writer's fertile imagination. For centuries scientists and scholars alike have been dimly aware that the existence of 'mind over matter' is a distinct possibility. Even before the Industrial Revolution, and the resurgence of interest in the methods of science which it brought, there were stories of people gifted with very peculiar and miraculous abilities. Tales of houses infested by very peculiar manifestations were common as well. According to the records of the Catholic Church, saintly people — such as St Teresa of Avila and St Joseph of Copertino — were able to levitate and float in the air before scores of witnesses. Likewise, even the writers of the Egyptian papyri told of houses plagued by demons who threw objects around and broke furniture.

By the Middle Ages, scientists were well aware that some psychic force hidden within man's mind could be coaxed out into the open by direct willpower. For example, in his posthumously published *Sylva Sylvarum*, Francis Bacon (1561-1626) wrote that there was a physical force within man's imagination that could be tested, '. . . upon things that have the lightest and easiest motions . . . as upon the sudden fading or coming up of herbs; or upon their bending one way or other . . . or upon the casting of dice.'[6] But it has been only recently that scientists have been trying to demonstrate mind over matter experimentally in the laboratory. This search has now gone on for over a century. Mind over matter is not a philosophical issue, to be debated with hypotheses, rebuttals, theorems or polemics. It is a theory that can be scientifically tested, and the results of these experiments and observations constitute the core of this volume.

Psychokinesis, or 'mind over matter', is, of course, only one of a variety of interrelated phenomena generally called 'paranormal' or 'psychic'. Parapsychologists study psychokinesis (PK) along with telepathy, clairvoyance, precognition, haunted houses, and other bizarre and little understood phenomena. Even though PK is a physical phenomenon, while ESP is a purely mental one, there is an intrinsic relationship between the two; that is why they are lumped together. Barriers do not seem to limit the efficacy of either ESP or PK, which can freely penetrate obstacles of any sort. Neither does distance have any great effect on either phenomenon. But, most importantly, both phenomena represent some sort of interaction between the mind and the material world. This is probably the most striking parallel between the two. When someone is making use of ESP, they are showing that the mind can directly interact with another mind, brain, or directly with the physical world. Psychokinesis merely demonstrates that the mind can *influence* the outside world.

J. B. Rhine, who is generally considered the founder of modern parapsychology, makes this point forcefully in his book *The Reach of the Mind,* where he writes,

> The PK hypothesis is a logical follow-up of the ESP work itself. In the clairvoyant perception of objects there has to be some operation between the mind and the material objects. Each must have an effect on the other; at least that is the way all known reactions work. The mind, therefore, does something to the object, even though that something be too slight to be observed. The clairvoyance test, of course, was not designed to discover any such effect; what was needed was a means of measurement sensitive enough to register any such mental effect on the physical object. We would expect psychophysical interaction to show effects on the physical side as well as on the psychical. Why not extra*motor* as well as extrasensory perception?[71]

One of Rhine's dice-rolling experiments at Duke University in the 1930's. (Mary Evans Picture Library)

Rhine's first attempts to demonstrate scientifically the existence of PK at Duke University, where he had set up his laboratory in the 1930s, was through rolling dice. Subjects activated dice thrown in mechanically-driven apparatuses, while trying to influence selected die faces to come up more often than chance could account for. These tests, which will be described in more detail later, were ultimately successful.

Dice-rolling psychokinetic effects are, however, only a measure of PK. The effect is meagre. We don't really directly witness it, we only *infer* it through the application of statistics and other measurements. The only way we know that PK has been operating is to run the test over and over again. Then we can measure how often the dice have departed from the way that they should have landed normally, i.e. at random. On the other hand, reports of much more sensational PK effects have been placed on record. Here is a small selection of them:

> Some people possess the ability to move objects across counters and tables through PK. This psychic power is not limited to matchboxes or other small objects. Some psychics have, under good control and observation, caused tables to levitate, produced psychic pictures on photographic film, swung pendulums in sealed containers, or even caused temperatures in the experimental room to fluctuate.

> There is now evidence that some people can use PK to help animals and plants recover from biological damage. This phenomenon has given the concept of psychic healing its first scientific credence.

> During the 1970s parapsychologists were besieged by people who claimed that they could cause metal to break, bend or contort merely by stroking it.

> Even cases of teleportation, where an object suddenly appears in a sealed room as though penetrating solid matter, are on record. Such effects often occur during so-called 'poltergeist' attacks.

The various forms of PK are almost limitless. But all of these effects point in the same direction . . . that within all of us may be a physical force, the existence of which would require the laws of physics, as we now conceive them, to be revised.

1.

Spontaneous Psychokinesis

Shortly after the turn of the century, the mother of Camille Flammarion — the famous French astronomer — placed the following account on record:

> One night . . . in our bedroom, we were awakened by a great noise; we had heard a mirror on the mantelpiece fall down, as well as your father's watchstand. I got up, and found that the mirror had fallen upon the hearth; the watch had been thrown upon the floor on one side and the watchstand on the other. I thought that everything was broken, and, most annoyed, I must say, I went back to bed without further investigation. In the morning when we got up, we found that nothing had been broken.[28]

So far there is nothing out of the ordinary in this account since you might be thinking that mirrors fall from walls all the time. But it is the sequel to this episode that is so unusual.

'The same morning the postman brought us a letter,' continued Mme. Flammarion, 'telling us of the death of your Aunt Boyet, your father's sister, who had died that very night, in Montigny. What did this manifestation mean? The coincidence is, at least, strange.'

Death coincidences

This account is an example of one of the commonest forms of spontaneous psychokinesis. Scattered throughout not only the literature of parapsychology but throughout history itself, are reports of strange psychic happenings that tend to occur at the exact moment someone

Camille Flammarion, the eminent French astronomer, for whom psychic forces were a serious scientific phenomenon. (Mary Evans/Society for Psychical Research)

dies. These curious 'death coincidences' come in many guises. Odd noises, violent poundings, flying or spontaneously-breaking objects, mysterious clock-stoppings — these are all types of psychokinetic effects that have been recorded by the more than startled witnesses. Before modern parapsychology began delving into these reports, it was automatically assumed that these eerie effects were caused by the souls of the dead, who were seeking to announce their demises to their friends and relatives.

Several such cases were collected by Camille Flammarion and are included in his monumental three-volume study, *Death and its Mystery*, which even today remains as an authoritative source of information on these types of cases. One of his correspondents, for instance, wrote to him about a friend of his who had been so ill that he had not been able to attend his seminary classes. His illness lingered on for months. Now each student had his own personal nail pounded into the wall of the classroom upon which he could hang his coat and hat. The sick student's space was therefore always vacant during this critical time, so one day a fellow student decided to take advantage of the vacancy by placing his own hat on the nail. As the correspondent explained:

> Now one day between eleven o'clock and noon, while the entire class was attentively following the professor's course, the hat on the absent pupil's nail suddenly began to turn, without the least plausible reason being discernable. This motion was so energetic, and lasted for so long (almost a minute) that it drew the pupils' attention, and even the professor's, and made much an impression that they talked of it the whole day.[28]

Later that afternoon a cable arrived announcing that the ill student had died at that very time.

Directly observable psychokinetic effects are not the only type of death coincidences that have been reported in the literature. Inexplicable sounds have also been quite commonly recorded. For example, one of Flammarion's acquaintances reported that one day his entire family was shocked by these incredible sounds during their evening prayers. He noted that 'an extraordinary noise made itself heard . . . as though the heavy counter had been violently shaken, making the scales and everything upon it resound noisily.' The family ran into the office, expecting to find something broken or at least in disarray. Everything there was in perfect order, but news arrived later that evening announcing the death of a relative.

Other death coincidences could be cited in which human cries were heard, footsteps stalked about, or shutters mysteriously jiggled. But before citing more of these fascinating anecdotes, let's turn to a more important issue. Just what do these phenomena mean and why do they occur? Even the first psychic investigators felt that these incidents were caused psychokinetically by the dying or deceased person. To them, these cases indicated that some component of the dead person's mind had survived death. The liberated soul had been able to travel to a relative's house to produce the physical manifestation. The reason, they believed, was the desire of the liberated soul to announce its earthly demise. These investigators were able to support their theory with some fascinating and valid points, since sometimes the psychokinetic event would repeat itself over and over until the witness finally 'got the message'. It certainly *looked* as though some sort of disembodied intelligence was the cause of the disturbances; and no one really attempted to delve into them further.[49]

New light on death coincidences

Unfortunately, no one took much interest in the study of these spontaneous psychokinetic events after Flammarion published his work, until experimental ESP and PK research was well under way at Duke University. It was only then that parapsychology began looking back at these cases and collecting new ones. The one researcher chiefly responsible for renewing interest in the subject was Dr Louisa Rhine, the wife and co-worker of Dr J. B. Rhine.[74] She, however, soon formulated an entirely different theory about the nature of death-coincidence PK — and one that radically differed from those proposed by earlier researchers who tended to take them at face value. This new understanding of spontaneous PK was partly an outgrowth of the Rhines' research on extrasensory perception.

By the 1940s, experimental research on ESP and psychokinesis was well under way at Duke University, and Dr Rhine began thinking that it was about time that someone at the lab started looking into cases of ESP and PK reported from everyday life. He soon interested his wife in this project.

Mrs Rhine was primarily interested in the types of psychic experiences reported by ordinary people who didn't consider themselves in any way psychic; so she started analysing and cataloguing the many cases that were being sent in almost daily to the Duke University parapsychology laboratory. These cases were being reported by people who were usually simply curious about their experience. Mrs Rhine soon discovered that many types of psychic occurrences seemed to group themselves around death. She uncovered many cases in which friends and relatives of a dying person telepathically dreamed about the event or experienced sudden intuitions, 'hunches', or formed mental pictures of the critical event.

But Mrs Rhine was also able to collect several accounts of psychokinetic incidents that seemed to announce the deaths. These cases were very similar to the type of reports collected by Flammarion years before. This created a curious puzzle in Mrs Rhine's mind, for she was sure that there was a connection between these ESP cases and the PK ones. Why, she wondered, was ESP the vehicle of communication in one instance, while PK occurred in some of the others?

Mrs Rhine resolved the dilemma by suggesting that it was the mind of the *witness* that was actually producing the PK events. She didn't believe at all that the dying or deceased person's psyche or surviving mind had anything to do with them, and she thus rejected the viewpoints of many earlier researchers who had studied these cases. Her idea was that death-coincidence PK occurs when the mind first receives a telepathic or clairvoyant message about a death. It then 'externalizes' the information by producing — unconsciously, of course — the actual physical (PK) event.

This theory admittedly makes good sense from a purely parapsychological perspective. Even the cases themselves contained direct suggestions pointing to this process. For example, Mrs Rhine reports a case in which a man passionately fond of money heard noises like coins being tossed about when a relative died. A child with an inordinate fondness for birds heard bird cries at the moment of a death occurring miles away. Note how, in each of these instances, the PK effect seemed to echo the witnesses' own interests. The fact that PK moulds itself to fit the emotional preoccupations of the witnesses would indicate, argued Mrs Rhine, that he or she is the actual producer of the effect.

Mysterious clock-stoppings

Even though PK effects that occur at death manifest in very personal ways, there is one type of death coincidence that occurs so often that it represents a phenomenon in its own right. No discussion of spontaneous PK can be complete without taking a detailed look at *the* most prevalent form of death coincidence . . . spontaneous clock stoppings.

There is a world-wide folk tradition that the clocks in a dying person's home will stop mysteriously when the death occurs. I am sure everyone reading these pages is familiar with the song about 'My grandfather's clock' that 'stopped short, never to run again, when the old man died.' This little song exemplifies the vast tradition associated with PK-induced clock phenomena. So let's look at a few cases.

The following incident is almost a classical example of the phenomenon. It was reported to Mrs Rhine by a man who was the proud owner of a gold pocket watch given to him by his brother:

> I took leave from my job and sat up nights to help my sister-in-law during the last two days of my brother's terminal illness. He breathed his last at six-twenty-five in the morning. I called the family immediately and we phoned for the doctor and the undertakers. At about seven-thirty we were sitting around a rush breakfast — my two brothers, the widow and the nurse.
>
> Arrangements had previously been made to be at the undertaking parlors at nine-thirty, so as the wall clock neared nine o'clock, I suggested it was about time . . . and my brothers made arrangements to get started for the funeral parlor. Some one asked me how much time we had, and I took out the pocket watch mentioned above, when, lo and behold, it had stopped at the exact minute of his death. I called the attention of those gathered around the table to the phenomenon and in order to show that it was no common occurrence, asked my brother to wind the watch to make sure it had not run down. It was three-quarters wound. [74]

There are probably many reasons why this type of PK clock-stopping is so common. They probably arise from the fact that there are both obvious and symbolic meanings communicated by the incidents. If the witness is using PK to learn about a death in response to a psychic message, it would seem likely that the witness would seek to bring his/her attention to the exact time of the death. Stopping a clock or watch would be the most overt way of getting the message across. On the other hand, the PK effect may be a symbolic reaction to the death. Everyone knows that an old euphemism for death is to say that 'his time has run out'. This phrase emphasizes the fact that we symbolically associate death with the stopping of time. These PK clock-stoppings are perhaps literal allusions to how we feel about death — i.e., that time has stopped for the recently deceased person. Nothing can be more final than the end of time, nor the finality of death, so the stopping of time is symbolic of the act of dying.

Spontaneous PK related to trauma

Not all cases of spontaneous PK focus solely on death, however. Examples of spontaneous PK can occur in response to other situations as well. Even some well-familiar clock cases illustrate this. In her book *ESP in Life and Lab*, Mrs Rhine cites one such rather revealing case. It was reported by a woman who had a psychic penchant for confusing her household clock:

> We have a clock over a hundred years old which belonged to my father before me and to his mother before him. A few years ago my parents were living with us, and the clock rested on the mantel in the front hall. We lived in a home in Chicago, Illinois.
>
> The day of mother's death in 1952 the clock stopped at the exact time of her passing. I rewound the clock and the next day it stopped at that exact time. It has never since stopped at that time. The clock uses more than twenty-four hours to run down before stopping, so that would eliminate its second stopping at that exact time from being run down.
>
> We were living in the same house about three years later when our eldest daughter's first baby was born. When my husband and I returned from the hospital, I noted that the clock had stopped at the exact moment the baby was born. I rewound the clock, and the following day it again stopped at that exact time. It has never again stopped at that time.
>
> A few years later, in 1956, we moved from Chicago to our present home in the suburbs about twenty miles distant. The clock was placed in the front hall. In 1958 our youngest daughter was married at our church in Chicago. When we returned home, the clock had stopped at the exact time the minister had pronounced them man and wife, as I had glanced at my wristwatch at that time. I rewound the clock, and it has never again stopped from being run down, as time proved it doesn't stop running in twenty-four hours after winding. It takes much longer. [74]

This case is probably telling us a great deal about the PK process. Even though the first incident was a conventional death coincidence, the number of repeated clock-stoppings is most revealing. It indicates that the narrator was the likely source of the PK and that we can sometimes use PK unwittingly in our daily lives. It would seem likely that, in this case, Mrs Rhine's informant — for some psychological reason — habitually used psychokinesis in order to make herself aware of emotionally meaningful events taking place within her family. Note again how such a process suggests that the PK was actually the outgrowth of a telepathic communication. The above incidents also demonstrate that we can even project PK over great distances.

In order to prove more conclusively that spontaneous PK effects emerge from the witness's own mind, Mrs Rhine has also pointed out that very similar phenomena occur in situations *other* than death.[73] For example:

> One woman reported to her that a dish literally jumped out of the cupboard as she was washing and stacking them. It landed noisily on a stack of plates below. The woman experienced a sudden intuitive flash that something had happened to her hospitalized sister. She later learned that her sister had haemorrhaged during an operation at that very time. She almost died, but thankfully recovered.

> An Arkansas couple reported that they had once been jolted from sleep when a light bulb exploded in their bedroom. Little did they realize that, at the same time, a farm owned by close relatives was burning to the ground.

> One perplexed woman wrote to Mrs Rhine about a lamp in her room that couldn't decide whether it was going to turn itself on or turn itself off. The witness couldn't find any normal cause for the lamp's peculiar behaviour. She learned only later that her husband had been involved in an accident at the time of the incident. He was shaken up, but unhurt.

These types of cases may not seem very dramatic, though no doubt they were very startling to the percipients who were involved. They are certainly a far cry from the levitating tables or hovering pieces of furniture produced by the great psychics of the past or during poltergeist outbreaks. But always remember that these effects might only be the tip of a great iceberg. These reports are also very important to our understanding of the PK process; for to quote Mrs Rhine again, 'For that matter, the sparks from Franklin's electric machine were small too, compared to the power of electricity in a thunderstorm.'

This is not to say, however, that all expressions of PK in every day life are so trivial. Sometimes these spontaneous psychokinetic outbursts can be incredibly powerful. The great explorer of the mind C. G. Jung, the celebrated Swiss psychoanalyst, was able to testify to that fact. He readily admitted in later life that his home once became the scene of some stormy PK activity at that time during his student days when he was preoccupied with psychic studies. Writing in his autobiographical *Memories, Dreams, Reflections,* he admitted that these youthful encounters with PK were 'destined to influence me profoundly'. One incident so confounded him that, many years later, he corresponded with Dr J. B. Rhine about it:

> One day I was sitting in my room, studying my textbooks. In the adjoining room, the door to which stood ajar, my mother was knitting. That was our

dining room, where the round walnut dining table stood. The table had come from the dowry of my paternal grandmother, and was at this time about seventy years old. My mother was sitting by the window, about a yard away from the table. My sister was at school and our maid in the kitchen. Suddenly there sounded a report like a pistol shot. I jumped up and rushed into the room from which the noise of the explosion had come. My mother was sitting flabbergasted in her armchair, the knitting fallen from her hands. She stammered out, 'W-w-what's happened. It was right beside me!' and stared at the table. Following her eyes, I saw what happened. The table top had split from the rim to beyond the center and not along any joint; the split ran right through the solid wood. I was thunderstruck. How could such a thing happen? A table of solid walnut that had dried out for seventy years — how could it split on a summer day in the relatively high degree of humidity characteristic of our climate? If it had stood next to a heated stove on a cold, dry winter day, then it might have been conceivable. What in the world could have caused such an explosion? 'There certainly are curious accidents,' I thought. My mother nodded darkly. 'Yes, yes,' she said . . ., 'that means something.' Against my will I was impressed and annoyed with myself for not finding anything to say.

Some two weeks later I came home at six o'clock in the evening and found the household — my mother, my fourteen-year-old-sister and the maid — in a great state of agitation. About an hour earlier there had been another deafening report. This time it was not the already damaged table; the noise had come from the direction of the sideboard, a heavy piece of furniture dating from the early nineteenth century. They had already looked all over it, but had found no trace of a split. I immediately began examining the sideboard and the entire surrounding area, but just as fruitlessly. Then I began on the interior of the sideboard. In the cupboard containing the bread basket I found a loaf of bread, and beside it, the bread knife. The greater part of the blade had snapped off in several pieces. The handle lay in one corner of the rectangular basket, and in each of the other corners lay a piece of the blade. The knife had been used shortly before, at four-o'clock tea, and afterward put away. Since then no one had gone to the sideboard.[43]

Dr Jung's experiences reveal that not all outbreaks of PK are restricted to single events. Sometimes our PK abilities will erupt from our minds and bodies without our realizing it. Released is a virtual attack of PK manifestations: objects will be hurled about, furniture will be overturned, lights will be smashed, walls will be pounded upon, and countless other types of disturbances will erupt. These psychokinetic storms constitute the phenomenon of the poltergeist, to which we will now turn.

Assessing the evidence

Death coincidence and spontaneous PK represent the first stepping-stone in our survey of the evidence for such a force. They represent weak evidence in one respect, since they are only anecdotal reports. They constitute a log of fascinating stories, but such accounts — while inherently credible — would hardly impress the sceptic. What *is* so impressive about these cases, however, is that they conform to patterns. Despite the fact that Camille Flammarion's work was conducted in Europe at the turn of the century, his cases read no differently from those catalogued in the United States by Dr Louisa Rhine four decades later. The actual number of 'clock-stopping' cases alone is astonishing. So, while not impressive by scientific standards, these cases do point tentatively to the existence of psychokinesis.

2.

The Evidence for
the Poltergeist

On November 25, 1974, the wire services in just about every major city in the United States carried a bizarre and unbelievable story. It concerned a little house in the small town of Bridgeport, Connecticut, that had suddenly become haunted. The witnesses were claiming that knick-knacks were being tossed about the house, that silverware was shooting around like make-shift missiles, and that a television set had jumped from a table by itself. The news story closed with the report that both police and clergymen were on the scene looking for a likely cause. Over a hundred onlookers had swarmed to the house like ants over a lump of sugar, hoping to see the events for themselves.

The rather banal denouement of the story came the next day, however, when it was stated in the *Los Angeles Times* that 'police today said that the unnatural happenings witnessed by police and firemen in a private home were a hoax perpetrated by a ten-year-old girl. Detective Capt. Anthony Fabrizi said that the girl, Meredith Goodin, adopted by Mr and Mrs Gerald Goodin admitted tossing around furniture in the home when no one was looking.'

The case was far from settled, however, since not everyone was happy with the police department's official explanation. The Rev William Charbonneaux was a Roman Catholic priest who had been called in by the family to observe the preternatural force at work. He was certainly not in the least impressed by the police statement. Rev Charbonneaux told reporters that he had deliberately checked the house for wires and trick devices during his first visit, but failed to uncover anything that looked suspicious. He also insisted that he had actually seen household objects move by themselves while little Meredith was under his direct observation. He explained how, on one occasion, the girl was standing right next to him when a heavy dresser suddenly started to move from behind her. The girl was holding a bracelet in both hands at the time. The priest also explained that a television set slid off a table and fell to the floor on another occasion when he was holding vigil and that Meredith was not even in the room at the time.

Mr and Mrs Goodin were left as perplexed as ever. One could hardly blame them. The police were claiming that the whole haunting was a fraud, while their priest was maintaining — just as staunchly — that it was genuine. The miracle-mongering crowds outside the house eventually sided with the police and finally dispersed, leaving the Goodins in peace. The police closed their files on the case and departed but the object-throwings continued nonetheless, and the Goodins were left wondering just what was happening to them.

Were the Bridgeport disturbances real or fake? Was some sort of psychokinetic force erupting in the house, or was little Meredith Goodin just a fraud? Revisiting the case today, over ten years later, we might be able to come up with some sort of solution.

The whole terrifying ordeal started for the Goodins on 23 November. Gerald Goodin had come home from work to his wife, Laura, and had spent an enjoyable evening with his wife and adopted daughter. But, later that night, the entire family heard peculiar pounding noises emanating from the walls of the house. The knockings were not stationary but moved freely from one room to another.

It was not too long after the rappings began that various household items began moving by themselves. It was eight o'clock the next morning when Mr Goodin, still in his bedroom, heard a crashing noise from an adjoining room. He rushed onto the scene to find that a table had fallen over, and other tables and chairs followed suit as the bewildered factory worker looked on. The Goodins were so unnerved by the events that they called in two friends, Harold and Mary Hoffman. By the time the couple arrived the Goodin household looked as though it had been singled out by a tornado. The couple later testified that cutlery, dishes, and furniture were scattered about the house in total disarray. It was obvious that *something* had been flinging every conceivable item in the house about in a fury.

Several other witnesses observed the events that day as well. An off-duty policeman happened to be passing by just as the Goodins were trying to size up their situation. They quickly flagged him down and beseeched him to come inside, hoping that he could be of help. Policeman John Holsworth answered the frightened call — and became the first disinterested party actually to watch the antics in progress. He later testified that, 'I saw the heavy refrigerator lift slowly off the floor, turn, and then set down again. There was no one else around. The big TV set seemed to float in the air and crash to the floor.'

By noon that day police, the fire department, and various well-wishers were arriving at the scene. They were all searching for an explanation for the outbreak. One officer even watched as shelves in the house vibrated, broke loose, and flew into the air. It did not take police long to find a mundane explanation that they could report to the media though. Bridgeport's superintendent of police announced the next day that the Goodins' daughter was the culprit and had hoaxed the whole affair.

Even the police couldn't get by with that one, since their own officers disputed the explanation. The police withdrew from the case, nonetheless, even though the disturbances were continuing to plague the house. The Goodins eventually wired their furniture to the floor and began making plans to move.

In re-reading all the collected testimony on the Bridgeport case today, it still seems impressive. There were over forty visitors to the house who witnessed the outbreak; while some of them thought the entire affair was a fake, many others were equally sure that some supernatural force was rampaging in the Goodin home. Some of these witnesses included fire and police officials.

The Goodins were certainly not a unique family, and nor were they the first family suddenly to find itself in the middle of such a psychic eruption. Reports of homes besieged by inexplicable noises, object-throwings, and even more bizarre phenomena, have been recorded for centuries and from every part of the world. So let's go back further and examine a similar report which also came from the east coast of the USA.

Back in March 1958, similar reports were carried about a house in Seaford, Long Island.[77] The home belonged to Mr and Mrs James Herrmann who reported that they had seen objects moving about the house, bottles propelling from countertops and popping their tops, and furniture shifting around the floor. Their first reaction was to call in the police, but they could offer the Herrmanns no explanation for the outbreak. They did note, however, that their son, twelve-year-old Jimmy, seemed linked to the phenomena. The odd displays seemed only to occur when young Jimmy was home and awake, so the police grilled him intensely for a confession. The boy only cried and insisted that he was not responsible.

Despite police and several scientific investigations, the Herrmanns were given no reprieve from, nor explanation for, the nightmare. Bottles kept crashing into walls, while their furniture kept moving about as noisily as ever. Only then did news accounts of the Seaford disturbances come to the attention of Dr J. B. Rhine at the Duke University Parapsychology Laboratory. He quickly dispatched Dr J. G. Pratt and W. G. Roll, two researchers working at the lab, to the scene of the action. They could not come up with a normal cause for the incidents either, but after examining witnesses and weighing the evidence they diagnosed the Seaford case as a possible *poltergeist*.

Poltergeist is a German word which roughly translates as 'noisy ghost'. These outbreaks represent the next step in our study of psychokinesis.

The pattern of the poltergeist
So just what is a poltergeist?

Poltergeist disturbances are a form of spontaneous PK which usually erupts within a family setting. Such an unfortunate family will suddenly find itself victimized by any number of a vast range of manifestations. Raps will resound over the house, objects will move or fly about by themselves, furniture will shift position, objects will disappear and reappear mysteriously, fires will erupt, rocks will bombard the house, and so on. The poltergeist will harass the family with only one phenomenon in some cases, but will resort to a sort of combined attack strategy in others.

Poltergeist disturbances are also invariably linked *directly* with the family undergoing the attack. The phenomena will even follow them should they flee their house. Poltergeists also usually focus on one particular member of the household and this person will generally be an adolescent. These victims either become the focus of the attacks, or the phenomena will occur only when they are present and awake. If they are sent away from the family, for example, the outbreaks will most likely abate, but they will occur again when these focal agents return. Luckily, though, poltergeist infestations are usually brief and rarely last more than a few weeks to a couple of months.

The poltergeist is, nevertheless, anything but stereotyped and each case will be marked by its own peculiarities. The Goodins and Herrmanns were victimized by wild and unruly object-throwing poltergeists. This is perhaps the most common form that the outbreaks take, and the type most familiar to the general public. But there are actually many other specific types of poltergeist as well. So, before trying to understand the nature of the poltergeist, let's first take a look at five different additional types: rapping poltergeists, stone-throwing poltergeists, teleporting poltergeists, water poltergeists and fire poltergeists.

Rapping poltergeists

A typical rapping poltergeist made a nefarious appearance in the little German town of Pursruck in November 1970, continuing on well into the next year.[9] The scene of the infestation was an old schoolhouse which had been converted into an apartment building where two girls, Helga (aged thirteen) and Anna (aged eleven) were staying with their grandmother. Tappings were heard in the building after a member of a family living downstairs died, but these noises faded out after a few weeks and nothing more apparently happened that year.

The poltergeist began its real siege in May 1971. Raps, scraping noises, and sawing sounds could be heard in the elderly woman's apartment each night after the girls had retired. The noises were not stationary since they sometimes came from under the girls' beds and at other times erupted from cupboards and doors all over the apartment. They became so loud that onlookers claimed that they sounded like machine gun fire.

The first outside investigator to confront this poltergeist was Rev Jakob Wolfsteiner, a local village priest, who reported that:

> In the evening of June 9, 1971, I went to Pursruck with the agreement of the parents and the children of the family R. I took along my Contaflex camera with long distance objective, and electric flashlight, and a tape recorder. The girls were in their beds. In the first minutes, they were covered with their blankets, holding their hands folded on their foreheads. Later on, the girls' father took away the blankets so that their feet and their whole body (sic) would be seen. Tappings were to be heard . . . I observed the girls in the light of an electric torch. Tappings appeared when the girls lay completely quiet in their beds and went on when I spoke to them. After these adventures I was definitely convinced that the girls could not possibly have caused the phenomena with their hands or other parts of their bodies.

The priest responded by calling in a psychologist so that a clinical examination could be made of the girls. The psychologist, in turn, quickly discovered that the raps had begun after Anna had been frightened by a series of nightmares. These dreams concerned a man who would stand by her bed shaking snakes at her, which indicated to him that Anna was having psychological difficulties coping with her sexual development. It also suggested that the poltergeist outbreak itself was linked to the girl's problem.

It was also at this time that the Pursruck case came to the attention of Professor Hans Bender, a German psychologist, who then headed a division of parapsychology at the University of Freiburg. Bender was able to hear the raps for himself when he arrived in Pursruck. Unfortunately, though, the poltergeist soon degenerated when the girls, managing to overcome their fears, began faking the raps themselves. This unfortunate development did not totally undermine the value of the earlier testimony in the case and Bender left satisfied that it was at least partially genuine.

Reports of so-called rapping poltergeists read amazingly alike. A similar case occurred in the California community of Yucaipa in 1965, where it plagued the home of Mr and Mrs Kenneth Cannon and their three children.[5] Not only did the entire house shake from the blows, but objects would fall or fly from shelves as well. (So in this case we have a combination of a rapping poltergeist and an object-thrower.) Sometimes the poundings were so horrendous that the walls of the house would actually bulge out when struck. The family was soon nerve-wracked by the outbreak and it didn't help much either when gas repairmen, water company investigators, architects and geologists all told them that they could not account for the extraordinary bangings.

The first parapsychologist to follow up on the case was Raymond Bayless, a Los Angeles-based psychical investigator who has spent some thirty-five years searching out hauntings and poltergeists. Bayless drove to Yucaipa when he first learned of the case and soon discovered that the noises centred on the Cannon's twelve-year-old son Billy. Bayless was fortunate enough to witness the raps for himself and was more than impressed. He reported that on one occasion:

> Billy, aged twelve, entered the living room from the kitchen and walked toward the hall archway. As the boy reached a position about three feet from the hallway entrance three violent blows sounded from the hallway and related area of the doorway to the boy's bedroom which is the first door to the left upon entering the hallway. When the phenomena occurred the girl [Billy's sister] was continuing toward her room which entered to the left at the end of the hall. She did not enter her room until after the pounding. The blows were extremely loud and literally shook the house.

Later that evening, though, Bayless clearly saw Billy pounding on the walls with his fists. So here again we find a genuine case which contained a fraudulent element as well.

Stone-throwing poltergeists

From rapping poltergeists it isn't too much of a conceptual leap to stone-throwing ones. Object-throwers, as I mentioned earlier, are perhaps the most common form of poltergeist, and one of the most common types of object-throwing poltergeists is the psychic stone-thrower. During their attacks, stones — and often nothing else — will constitute the projectiles. Sometimes the stones will bombard *only* the outside of the house, i.e., periodic onslaughts of literally hundreds of stones will fall on the roof or catapult up against the sides of the structure for days at a time. These stones have sometimes been seen falling in zig-zag motions, and sometimes they will not bounce when they strike the ground. Stones falling abnormally slowly have often been noted as well, and it is not rare to find the stones warm to the touch.

One of the most celebrated stone-throwing poltergeists ever recorded was the Big Bear, California, case of 1962.[5] The scene of the action was the mountain residence of the Lowe family, which included an adopted daughter as well as several natural children. Family members and several sheriff's deputies witnessed the showers during the several days that the attacks lasted. The rocks would just suddenly appear over the house and then 'float' down and strike the roof. The local sheriffs tried to blame the disturbance on some prankster hiding near the property and armed with a slingshot, but they could never find the culprit even though they scoured the area. In fact, one rock shower even damaged a deputy's car! Nor could they ever explain how the rocks could fall in slow-motion from the sky.

The Lowe family could not handle the ordeal, and eventually packed up their belongings and moved. Two college students were the next to rent the cabin and, even as they helped the Lowes remove the last vestiges of their possessions, watched the uncanny falls of rocks. Somehow the Lowes' move vanquished the poltergeist. A few more stones fell . . . and the case was over.

Even more fascinating than this type of rock-throwing poltergeist is another form, which I like to call the 'indoor stone-thrower'. These cases are even more bizarre since the rocks will suddenly and mysteriously appear and fly about *inside* the house. A good example of such a case was reported by W. G. Grottendieck shortly after the turn of the century.[76]

Grottendieck was a Dutch traveller who was persecuted by a poltergeist for just one night in the jungles of Sumatra. He explains in his detailed report how he had settled down in a hut, no doubt expecting to pass a peaceful and uneventful evening. But the poltergeist had different ideas:

> I put my bullsack and mosquito netting on the wooden floor and soon fell asleep. At about one o'clock at night I half awoke, hearing something fall near my head outside the mosquito curtain on the floor. After a couple of minutes I completely awoke and turned my head half around to see what was falling on the floor. They were *black stones* from one-eighth to three-quarters of an inch long. I got out of the curtain and turned up the kerosene lamp that was standing on the floor at the foot of the bed. I saw then that the stones were falling through the roof in a parabolic line. They fell on the floor close to my head-pillow. I went out and awoke the boy (a Malay-Pelamdang) who was sleeping on the floor in the next room. I told him to go outside and examine the jungle up to a certain distance. He did so whilst I lighted up the jungle by means of a small 'ever-ready' electric lantern. At the same time that my boy was outside the stones did not stop falling. My boy came in again, and I told him to search the kitchen to see if anybody could be there. He went to the kitchen and I went inside the room again to watch the stones falling down. I knelt down near the head of my bed and tried to catch the stones while they were falling through the air towards me, but I could never catch them; it seemed to me that they *changed their direction* in the air as soon as I tried to get hold of them. I could not catch any of them before they fell to the floor. Then I climbed up the partition-wall between my room and the boy's and examined the roof just above it from which the stones were flying. They came right through the 'kadgang' but there were no holes in the kadgang. When I tried to catch them at the very spot of coming out, I also failed.

Mr Grottendieck clearly suggests in his written account that the stones could not have entered the house in any normal way. So how, then, did they get in? It seems likely that they were somehow *teleported* there.

Teleporting poltergeists

Matter-through-matter, or teleportation, is a phenomenon which is also sometimes noted during more conventional poltergeist cases. It was especially well-witnessed during a poltergeist attack that erupted in Nickleheim, Germany, in 1968-9 where Dr Bender was, once again, on the scene. He was able to make a detailed investigation of the affair.[9]

The victims were a labourer, his wife and their thirteen-year-old daughter Brigitte. The poltergeist ran fairly true to form by first making

Stone-throwing is archetypal poltergeist phenomena. At Saint Quentin, France, in 1849 stones from outside the house pierced the window panes like bullets, instead of shattering them as would be normal. (Mary Evans Picture Library)

its presence known by rapping on doors and windows. These episodes lasted for a while before the unwelcome visitor turned to stone-throwing. First the rocks fell on the roof, but soon they began to appear right inside the house. These incidents mystified the family for several days before more conventional object-displacements began. The force threw furniture about, cracked eggs, tore clothing, and even positioned Brigitte's dolls in obscene poses!

The teleportations, aside from the mysteriously appearing rocks, began during the height of the frenzy. The first well-witnessed incident occurred when a priest was called in to bless the house. The family hoped that the ritual would banish the 'demon' attacking them, but no sooner had the clergyman read the sacred words over the house than a rock suddenly fell from the ceiling. It plopped to the floor in front of the startled onlookers, but did not bounce when it struck. The priest picked the stone up to examine it and found that it was warm.

Dr Bender also witnessed the poltergeist's teleporting ability when he arrived on the scene. In a report he made to the 1969 annual convention of the Parapsychological Association (which convened in New York), Bender explained exactly what happened during his visit. He reported how he was sitting with the family in the kitchen at the time, having hung his coat in a nearby wardrobe only moments before. Brigitte's mother had just gone to the window to see what was troubling a noisy cat outside. Soon she called to the researcher 'Your coat is outside the house carefully laid in the snow beside the staircase.'

Bender had the entire family under his personal observation at the time, but gave up his vigil and ran outside to check the excited woman's report. There he found his coat lying on a bed of snow without even a single footstep near it. He was sure that no member of the family could have manoeuvred the incident, since they had been in the house with him at the critical moment. The poltergeist had apparently stolen the coat from the wardrobe and placed it outside.

By this time, dozens of visitors were dropping in at the house hoping to see the manifestations. So when the poltergeist began to be shy, little Brigitte was more than willing to provide additional entertainment. She was soon caught faking the poltergeist phenomena and Bender's investigation came to a halt. When the children in an active case begin to fake, it is a sure sign that the real poltergeist has ebbed.

Watery poltergeists
So far we have been surveying only the more commonly reported types

of poltergeist cases. However, the poltergeist will sometimes resort to extremely bizarre forms of psychic persecution. The following cases represent one of the rarest forms of poltergeist attacks — i.e., the water poltergeist, in which the poltergeist precipitates water all over the house instead of throwing things about. Only a few such cases are on record, but the most noteworthy of them occurred in Methuen, Massachusetts, in 1963.[5]

The poltergeist started plaguing the Francis Martin family in October. It all started unexpectedly when they noticed a peculiar 'wet spot' on the wall of the television room in their apartment one evening while they were relaxing after a busy day. They heard a 'pop' like a firecracker going off, and a jet of water squirted from the wall! This almost humorous incident was only the beginning of what turned out to be quite an ordeal. Water was ejected from the walls almost continually over the next three days, and the Martins finally had to flee the apartment.

The water jets seemed to follow a particular pattern. Mrs Martin, who personally saw several of these water spurts, later told researchers that, 'The water jets out for about twenty seconds and then they'll be a fifteen minute interval and it starts someplace else. There's a little tremor, and then a 'shoosh', and then the water.'

Local officials were soon on the scene to investigate. A crew of firemen checked the roof of the complex for any leakage that could be contributing to the nuisance. They were doubly bewildered since no other apartment residents reported any plumbing malfunction, and they left the building just as puzzled as before.

The water popping did not stop when the Martins fled, but followed wherever they went. They first moved in with Mrs Martin's mother who lived in an apartment in a neighbouring town, but no sooner had they unpacked than water began jetting out of *five* rooms in that apartment. Fire and police officials were called in once again. By this time, however, one of the fire investigators began to suspect that perhaps the Martin's eleven-year-old daughter was responsible for the plague. He decided to watch her carefully and what he saw amazed him:

> At one time I was standing in such a position in the kitchen that I also had the pantry wall in my vision. The eleven year old girl was in the pantry at the time, but obscured from my vision. I heard her yell, 'There's the water again' and I quickly took in the pantry wall, and what I saw was either water leaving the wall, or bouncing off the wall . . .
> By this time there were twelve adults in the five room apartment.

There were nine from the fire department, the landlord, Mr Martin and his mother-in-law. The water condition was happening in every room in the apartment.

So the little girl was apparently not the *normal* source of the disturbances.

Since the water sprite seemed to be following them, the Martins decided to return to their own apartment, but their return heralded still more mysterious phenomena. Not only did water continue to pop out of the walls, but now the room's humidity fluctuated radically. The poppings continued even when the water supply to the entire building was turned off.

By this time the case had made quite a stir in the press. Fire officials and plumbing experts were doing everything in their power to discover a more normal explanation for the affair, but to no avail. The poor Martins also got stuck playing host to hundreds of curiosity seekers who were converging on their home. The police finally withdrew from the case arguing that the Martins' daughter *had* to be responsible for the affair, and the fire department retired soon after. Their 'official' explanation was that the water was accumulating in the apartment's insulation and was periodically bursting through a hole in the ceiling. Of course, they never tried to explain why the water followed the Martin family from apartment to apartment!

The source of the 'hole in the ceiling' theory actually came from the Martins themselves, so it was later learned. Wearied by the lengthy and fruitless investigations, the family contrived the story in order to put a stop to the whole mess. Luckily, the ploy worked. Interest in the case soon ebbed, the crowds dispersed, and after a while, the water poppings ceased. Thus ended the case of Methuen's water sprite, as mysteriously as it began.

Water poltergeists are probably the most infrequent of all such cases. The only other truly notable case was reported from Germany in 1972.[9] The scene of this poltergeist was a home in the little village of Scherfede, where a twelve-year-old girl lived with her parents. Small puddles of water began to form on the floor of the house in September. Plumbing experts were called in to check over the water pipes and heating systems, but were unable to find any cause for the precipitations. By October, though, the phenomena had taken on a new twist. Humid moist spots started to appear on the walls, and damp spots began appearing on the carpets. By 10 December the poltergeist had really begun its attack. Hans Bender, who later investigated the case, explains that:

In intervals of twenty to thirty minutes, big water puddles appeared in the drawing room of the house. The family K. — father, mother and a thirteen-year-old girl Kerstin — heard a splashing when they were in another room. Nothing happened when they were present, and no one has ever seen a pool in formation. Technicians came and admitted that they were completely puzzled and could not find any cause. Trickery was excluded by carefully observing the room in question. At 7:30 p.m. neighbors of the next-but-one house came and asked for help: floods of water had suddenly appeared on the second floor and were coming down the staircase. There was too much to mop up with floor cloths. Helpers formed an echelon and brushed it out of the house. They were still at work when an hour later help was claimed for the next house where unexplainable water pools and splashes appeared and, another hour later, the same happened in the adjoining house, the last one of the row. This continued, more or less intensely, for three days.

When the water main was cut off to the K's house, the water gushes continued nonetheless. Building technicians, geologists and hydrologists all converged on the scene in due course, but ended up scratching their heads in bewilderment.

It was at this time that Dr Bender was called in on the case by a local magistrate. He and his colleagues soon realized that little thirteen-year-old Kerstin was probably the paranormal source of the infestation. The water seemed to precipitate only in those homes she had visited . . . especially if she had used the lavatories there. The one house on the block that Kerstin had never visited was the only one to escape the watery contagion.

Fiery poltergeists

Some poltergeists seem to be self-restrictive, and like to rely on only one paranormal effect. The Methuen and Scherfede cases are representative, since *only* water was used for the attacks. Fire-igniting is another form of poltergeistic nuisance, but an even more vicious and destructive one.

Fire poltergeists, as the name implies, delight in setting off fires in the houses they are persecuting — and will continue to ignite them one after the other. Forty to fifty fires a day are not unheard of in some of these cases, and sometimes even non-flammable objects will burst into flames during the outbreak. Fire officials are usually called in when such a case strikes, but no normal cause for the blazes is found.

The most notable fire poltergeist incident was probably the Macomb, Illinois, case of 1948.[31] The horror started in the first week of August when the Willey family noticed spots appearing on the wallpaper of their farmhouse. These brown spots would get hotter and hotter and then — in an instant — burst into flames. The fires were witnessed by the entire household, including Willey himself, his wife, his brother-in-law, his nephew (aged eight) and his niece (aged nine).

The brown spots and fires erupted all day long and the family had to keep on their toes to stem each new blaze before it got out of control. Neighbours soon came to the aid of the puzzled family with buckets in hand; and pans of water actually had to be stationed throughout the house as a safeguard. The family's first response to the blazes was to call in the fire department, and inspectors were on the scene in no time. Their advice? Stripping the wallpaper off the walls was the only thing they could suggest, but denuding the walls made little difference. The fires just burst forth from the walls anyway and even the ceiling had its share. 'The whole thing is so screwy and fantastic that I'm almost ashamed to talk about it,' the local fire chief admitted to the press.

The mysterious fires expanded their scope during the second week in August. Now they began igniting outside the house. The porch flared up; an ironing board outside was set on fire; and, back inside, the curtains were badly burned. Fire officials estimated that over two hundred fires plagued the Willey house during the course of the epidemic. By 14 August — two weeks after the brown spots first appeared — it was no longer any use to even try to contain the blaze. The house was finally consumed in flames.

The Willeys were left homeless and hapless, so they took up rather rugged living accommodation in a large tent that they pitched on their property. But despite the fact that they no longer had a home in which to live, the fires still did not abate. The very day after their house was destroyed, the barn burned down. Two days after that the flames destroyed the milkhouse, tried to burn up the chicken house, and finally succeeded in burning down a second barn on the property. The only things that were left of the Willey farm by the end of the siege were six outhouses. It would seem that this poltergeist had a great respect for personal privacy.

The nature of the poltergeist
Luckily, though, the study of the poltergeist entails more than merely cataloguing case after case. Poltergeists represent one class of psychokinetic activity whose nature is fairly well understood.

By carefully reading the foregoing accounts, you should have noticed that adolescents were conspicuously present in almost every case. This pattern crops up in case after case. It would seem that somehow these adolescents are intrinsically related to the poltergeist. While it is true that adults will sometimes be the centre of the attack, this is much rarer. Even at the turn of the century psychic investigators were aware of this fact, although they erroneously assumed that the children were the culprits faking the disturbances. This was one theory that had at least a grain of truth to it, however, for these children were, in fact, the key by which we have begun to unlock the mystery of the poltergeist; but not for the reasons that the first parapsychologists assumed. It is more logical to suppose that these youngsters are producing the disturbances (although unconsciously) by PK. Far from being caused by spirits or demons, the real root of the poltergeist appears to be the poltergeist victim himself. But just why should our innate psychokinetic abilities take on such a monstrous dimension and form of expression?

Psychoanalysing the poltergeist has been a parapsychological pastime for years. Researchers have spent years trying to figure out what psychological motivation could cause innocent children to unleash such a horrible force. By subjecting them to psychological tests and clinical evaluations, psychologists and parapsychologists alike have now been getting to the root of the syndrome. Their studies have been telling us quite a lot about the dynamics of the poltergeist, what causes it to erupt, and what it is trying to express.

The fact that the poltergeist is a form of unconscious expression had been suspected for years. [29] Strong evidence that it is a form of psychological expression has had repeated confirmation, especially over the past few years. This evidence has been chiefly collected, presented and argued by two contemporary investigators — by W. G. Roll in the United States and by Dr Hans Bender in Germany. Both investigators have not only witnessed several modern cases, but in each instance they have amassed detailed psychological evaluations of the agents around whom the PK was focusing. Over two dozen profiles have been placed on record. It is more than revealing that most of these agents seem to share remarkably similar psychological profiles. Most were harbouring strong unconscious conflicts and hostilities; they revealed aggressions that were usually projected toward authority figures, such as their parents or employers. But to deal best with these conflicts, they simultaneously revealed an abnormally strong use of such defence mechanisms as repression, sublimation, and denial. These poltergeist victims, in other words, seem to be pushing strong underlying anger out of their conscious minds and back into the unconscious.

These profiles tell us a great deal about the nature and meaning of the poltergeist, since it would appear likely that these outbreaks are virtually born from this anger and represent an unconscious form of expression. When the victim can no longer control his intense unacknowledged anger, it looks as though the poltergeist is unleashed as a safety valve. The pent-up frustration becomes vented instantly! The poltergeist is also a safe method of expression, for the agent will remain perfectly unaware that he is causing the disturbance, and can therefore unwittingly express his hostility without guilt or the threat of punishment or reprisal.

This general theory also explains the psychological meaning behind the antics of the poltergeist. When a child becomes angry, he will invariably exhibit that anger by pounding on walls, throwing things in a rage, slamming doors, and even stealing. Notice how these are precisely the same acts upon which the poltergeist relies. It, too, likes to pound on walls, throw things and steal. So we might say that the poltergeist or PK force carries out the very same actions and nuisances that the agent would like to carry out consciously, but doesn't dare.

Despite the fact that we are beginning to understand the psychology of the poltergeist, we are still faced with a big question. Parapsychologists have still not even begun to fathom the mystery behind the physical force or energy upon which the poltergeist relies. How it can carry out seemingly impossible acts is just as great a mystery as it was when such outbreaks were blamed on spirits or devils. So our breakthrough in discovering the nature of this energy will obviously only come when we understand the nature of PK much better than we do at present. Despite this fact, poltergeist outbreaks represent some of the best evidence for psychokinesis known to parapsychology.

Assessing the evidence

Although poltergeists erupt outside the scientific laboratory, they do represent a remarkably well-witnessed phenomenon. The number of trained parapsychologists who have seen them in action (including myself) is growing, while other outbreaks have been witnessed by people — such as fire and police officials — not known for their credulity. The most common counter-theory which the sceptics like to bring forth is that these cases are, in fact, the result of fraud. This is called the 'naughty little girl' theory, but to apply this explanation invariably to all poltergeist cases would be both naïve and uncircumspect. Simply throwing an object by hand cannot account for objects flying in zig-zag motion, falling from the sky, or floating about. Yet all these rather bizarre types of movements have been adequately witnessed during several poltergeist cases. The sad fact remains, though, that the children in many infested homes do have a nasty habit of helping things out a bit! These transgressions have usually occurred toward the end of the outbreaks, and after the genuine PK has already been well-witnessed. The fact that the poltergeist agents tend to conform to specific psychological patterns also indicates that we are dealing with a genuine paranormal syndrome.

3.

The Golden Age of Mediumship

Even though Western culture has long accommodated tales of hauntings and poltergeists, scientists took little interest in these phenomena until 1848, when many newspapers in the United States began running stories about ghostly disturbances taking place in Rochester, New York. Beginning in March and April of that year, John D. Fox — along with his wife, and his two daughters — reported being continually annoyed by loud rappings from the walls of their Hydesville cottage. Neighbours were summoned and they too heard the rappings. Eventually the Foxes worked out a code with the raps and began communicating — as they supposed — with the intelligence which was purportedly stirring up the ruckus. This intelligence claimed to be the spirit of an itinerant salesman who had been murdered in the cottage by a previous tenant. The claim was never substantiated, but some newspapers were soon claiming that communication with the dead had been established. Other papers were less friendly to the report.

There can be little doubt that some sort of intelligence actually did lie behind the poundings. For instance, the raps could intelligently answer questions. Many of the Foxes' neighbours testified how they had challenged the raps to tell them how many children they had, or to rap out their ages. To their utter astonishment, the raps would often answer correctly. What were the New York townsfolk to make of all this?

The science of psychology was still in its pre-natal stages in 1848. The force of the unconscious was hardly realized and any odd 'psychic' disturbance was liable to be explained away as the result of 'electricity', demons, or fraud. Looking back on the Hydesville episode today, many will feel that the Fox family was being invaded by a typical poltergeist — a poltergeist produced by one or both of the daughters. The townsfolk, however, believed that the Fox manifestations could only have been emanating from the dead. Although many devout Christians believed that the whole thing was the work of the devil, it was at this time that the religion of Spiritualism was proclaimed. This new sect claimed that communication with the dead was scientifically established and that anyone could talk to his dead friends and relatives merely by finding a suitable channel or medium. The Fox sisters became Spiritualism's first mediums and travelled the country demonstrating their raps and other wonders.

The spread of Spiritualism gave the impetus to the beginnings of scientific interest in the paranormal. Especially in England, many philosophers, scientists, and savants began wondering how much truth lay behind Spiritualism and its phenomena. So, some thirty years after Spiritualism spread to Great Britain, the Society for Psychical Research was founded in 1882 by these intellectuals. Their goal was impartially and critically to study reports of psychic phenomena and the people who claimed psychic abilities. The founders of the S.P.R. consisted of a wide assortment of people. Several Spiritualist leaders who were interested in critically appraising psychic phenomena made up one element, while the other main constituency consisted of a group of Cambridge scholars. This latter group felt that, through the study of psychic phenomena, they might answer many philosophical questions about the nature of man. The original Spiritualist element of the S.P.R. began to fall away, however, when it became apparent that the dominant Cambridge group had little interest in the purely cultist aspects of psychic phenomena.

Psychical research flourished nonetheless, and soon an American branch was founded. These two academic societies, one in England and the other in the United States, carried out most of the important scientific and scholarly parapsychological work throughout the world until the 1930s. It was about that time that the universities began taking over psychical research after Rhine made such a brilliant breakthrough with his experiments at Duke University.

During these golden years of psychical research, many scientists all over the world became intrigued with reports about people who had the ability to create raps, move objects psychokinetically, and produce other spectacular phenomena. During these years, too, many phenomenal physical mediums (i.e., psychics who specialized in producing psychokinesis) emerged from within the Spiritualist movement. Some of them were eager to prove their powers to the scientific world, and scientists in both Europe and the United States were soon flocking to investigate their claims.

The mediumship of D. D. Home

Probably the greatest of the early physical mediums to emerge from the Spiritualist camp was Daniel Dunglas Home. Home was born in 1833 near Edinburgh, Scotland. He was one of eight children, but he was not raised by his true parents. He emigrated to the United States with an aunt, who had decided to live in the state of Connecticut, when he was only nine years old.

It soon became apparent that Home was a peculiar lad. It was obvious that he was tubercular as a child, a condition that would plague his health for years to come. Even as a youngster he complained about seeing visions of the dead, but it was not until he was a teenager that the most important phase of his psychic development came. Objects started mysteriously moving about in his presence, and it soon appeared that a full-blown poltergeist was in the making. Since Home's relatives were a staunchly religious family, they, like so many people of this era, believed that all paranormal manifestations were the work of the devil. Even their own flesh and blood could be no exception to the rule, so they lost no time turning him out.

Luckily, though, news of Home's psychic abilities began to spread through New England. It was not long before scientists from several Eastern universities began holding sessions with him in order to study his psychokinetic powers. Home eventually developed an astounding array of PK abilities, all of which he believed were produced by spirits of the dead working through him. Tales of these powers were not merely empty claims, for scholars the world over tested him and witnessed his displays.

Today, even though Home has been dead for close to a century, we have an almost day-by-day account of his psychic feats. For between 1867-9, his constant companion was the young nobleman Lord Adare (who later became Earl of Dunraven). The enthusiastic young man kept a detailed diary of his sessions with Home, and also recorded the spontaneous PK that often occurred in his presence. These notes were eventually published as *Experiences in Spiritualism with D. D. Home*. The book was meant for private circulation only, but was later republished

Daniel Dunglas Home, using the test apparatus devised by Brookes in 1871, produced convincing evidence of his powers. (Mary Evans Picture Library)

during the 1920s. This volume contains some of the most detailed accounts we have of Home's powers.

A seance with Home

During a typical seance, Home and his experimenters or sitters would seat themselves around a table in fairly strong light. The light was rarely diminished as the sitting progressed. Home would first go into a state of trance and then the psychokinetic displays would begin. The following extract represents just a portion of a seance recorded by Adare for March 4, 1869. The setting was a cottage owned by Lord Adare's father on the coast of Kerry. The guests sat around a cloth-covered table while props, such as an accordion, were kept on hand so that the PK (or the 'spirits') would have some handy objects to manipulate:

> . . . we remained sitting for an hour and a quarter without any manifestations whatever. Mr Home said several times, 'I feel a strong influence all about

me; it is strange that there are no physical manifestations.' At last I proposed
that some of the party should leave the room, being certain that something
must be wrong. Blackburn and I went away. Mr Home remarked, 'A few
moments will shew whether their presence was the obstruction.' Still no
manifestations. He then said, 'Charlie, do you and Lawless go, and send the
others back.' Lawless went with the greatest reluctance. The door had hardly
closed when there were cold currents, vibrations, and raps. I returned and
was scarcely seated, when the alphabet was called for, and this message given:
'We love Freddy, but he is not in a state of mind or body conducive to manifestations.'*
Wynne fetched the accordion. Mrs Blackburn was very soon after touched
on the dress, and something became plainly visible moving under the table
cloth, along the edge of the table, raising up the cloth several inches, as would
be done were a hand and arm underneath [underneath it]. The hand was
visible on the cloth to Mr Home, and I once faintly perceived it. It touched
Mrs Blackburn's hand. I was touched on the ankle, and several times on
the knee. Miss Wynne's dress was strongly pulled. The table was beautifully
raised in the air, by three successive lifts, to the height of eighteen inches
or two feet. Mr Home then took the accordion, holding it under the edge
of the table with one hand, the other resting on the table; soon after it began
to sound, it played with considerable power as well as great delicacy,
something like a voluntary, with airs introduced. Then there were sounds
like echoes, so fine, as to be scarcely audible. The accordion was drawn
out towards Mrs Blackburn, but not put into her hand. I expressed a wish
that it might be played without being held by Mr Home, upon which he
withdrew his hand, placing it on the table; the instrument was just touching
the under edge of the table, where it remained, as it were, suspended. It
began playing very gently. He clapped his hands several times to shew that
he was not touching it. The playing soon ceased, and he took it again. Some
notes sounded out of tune, and I said, 'Either wrong notes are played in
the chord, or the accordion is out of tune.' 'Out of tune' was rapped out on
the instrument. It played again very finely, and with the tremolo effect, which
struck me exceedingly.

. . . Soon after this we all heard strong sounds which proceeded seemingly
from a large oblong writing table, which stood several feet from us; we could
perceive it moving; it stopped within a foot of our table, which then moved
up to it. We heard first one and then another drawer opened, on the side
of the table farthest from us, and a rustling sound as if stirring papers. After
a short pause, the following sentence was given, partly, if not wholly, (I forgot

---

* The sitters would call out the alphabet and a rap would resound at the
appropriate letter, or the table would tilt a certain number of times in order
to designate a certain letter. Using this procedure many messages could be
tediously communicated.

which) by tilting the table: *'We must cease, but not before praying God to bless you.'* We then adjourned. During the sitting the table was again lifted in the beautiful manner before mentioned, reminding me very much of the action of bellows of the organ while being filled; and it is very remarkable that this occurred, as will be seen in the foregoing description, just before the playing commenced.[25]

Psychokinesis did not only occur when Home was giving seances, but seemed to linger on afterwards as well. Lord Adare recounted several examples of these spontaneous 'linger' effects in his book. For example, he attended a particularly impressive seance with Home on July 26, 1868, in London. No sooner had the group seated itself than cold breezes gusted through the room; the seance table hoisted into the air; raps broke out over the entire room; and Home's trance became agitated. Lord Adare and Home returned to their apartment after this rather trying ordeal, but the PK kept on plaguing them:

> I arrived at home about half an hour before Home. Soon after we had gone to bed we both heard the hall door loudly slammed. I said, 'Oh, Dan, you have left the door open, and someone has come in!' He declared he had locked it, and put the chain up; however, we both got up and went down to see what was the matter. I found the hall door locked and the chain up, and the study and dining room doors both wide open. I went into the study and heard raps, I then went out to where Home was standing in the entry, and we heard raps on the floor. He said, 'Oh, I am sure it is dear Old Dr Elliotson.' 'Yes,' was rapped. I then said, 'In that case I suppose no burglars came in and we may go to bed again?' 'Yes,' was rapped. We went upstairs, Dr Elliotson following us rapping on the banisters and walking about the room, and raps in various places. Home carried on for a little time, asking questions and receiving answers to them by raps.[25]

Raps and table levitations were not the only phenomena which would highlight Home's seances. One of his more bizarre PK effects was to materialize phantom forms. These figures were usually vague apparitional forms and sometimes only part of the figure would be visible.

Another of Home's astounding abilities was fire-immunity. During some of his trances he would become immune to fire and heat. He could sometimes even transfer this ability to other people present at his demonstrations. Lord Adare was able to observe many instances of this phenomenon for which Home became understandably famous, and the following represents part of one of Adare's accounts dated November 1868:

He went to the fire, poked up the coals, and putting his hand in, drew out a hot burning ember, about twice the size of an orange; this he carried about the room, as if to shew it to the spirits, and then brought it to us; we all examined it. He then put it back in the fire and showed us his hands; they were not in the least blackened or scorched, neither did they smell of fire, but on the contrary of a sweet scent which he threw off from his fingers at us across the table. Having apparently spoken to some spirit, he went back to the fire, and with his hand stirred the embers into a flame; then kneeling down, he placed his face right among the burning coals, moving it about as though bathing it in water. Then, getting up, he held his finger for some time in the flame of the candle. Presently, he took the same lump of coal he had previously handled and came over to us, blowing upon it to make it brighter. He then walked slowly round the table, and said, 'I want to see which of you will be the best subject. Ah? Adare will be the easiest, because he has been most with Dan.' Mr Jencken held out his hand, saying, 'Put it in mine', Home said, 'No, no, touch it and see', he touched it with the tip of his finger and burnt himself. [25]

Experimental research with D. D. Home

Home was more than willing to be tested by scientists. Perhaps the greatest scientist in Great Britain at that time was William Crookes, founder of the *Chemical News*, fellow of the Royal Society, and with several scientific inventions to his credit. He was extremely sceptical about Spiritualism and its mediums, and he decided to investigate their phenomena more to expose them than for any other reason. Crookes initiated a series of experiments with Home in 1871 which still stand, even today, as some of the most ingenious PK studies ever undertaken. [23]

The first of Crookes's reports on D. D. Home was published in the July 1870 issue of the *Quarterly Journal of Science*. It may have shocked the journal's rather conservative readers when, right at the onset of his paper, Crookes candidly admitted, 'These experiments appear conclusively to establish the existence of a new force in some unknown manner connected to the human organization which for convenience can be called the Psychic Force.' These remarks indicate that, unlike the Spiritualists, Crookes did not believe that spirits of the dead had much to do with Home's powers. He preferred to believe instead that the human body somehow houses a force that had previously evaded the notice of science. So he set about carefully measuring and investigating this force, using Home as his principal subject.

Since one of Home's most famous psychic abilities was to activate an accordion without touching it, this was a natural place for Crookes to start. The scientist began by constructing a special cage to guard the instrument. This cage was constructed of two wooden hoops (approximately two feet in diameter) around which insulated copper wire mesh was strung, thereby making a drum-shaped cylinder. The whole apparatus was especially designed so it could be slipped snugly under a table. That way no one could place a hand between the drum top and the underside of the table. However, a hand *could* be placed in the cage if it were pulled a few inches out from under the table.

The actual tests were run in Crookes's laboratory. Home was immediately successful at the accordion experiment and it played even while *floating* in the cage in full light. Crookes tried passing an electrical current through the mesh but it had little appreciable affect on the instrument.

In order to measure Home's psychic force, Crookes next built a peculiar weighing apparatus which consisted of a mahogany board, measuring thirty-six inches by one inch (90 by 2.5cm). The very end of one side of the board was bolted to a table; while the rest of it extended out and away from the table by about two and a half feet (80cm). Its end was hooked to a cable running to an overhead spring balance. If any pressure was exerted on the side of the board extending away from the table, this would be recorded by the balance. No pressure would be recorded if the subject merely pushed on the end of the board connected to the table, since the subject would be pressing fruitlessly onto the table itself.

During several experimental sessions, Crookes instructed Home to place the tips of his fingers on the section of the board bolted to the table. Home was often able to make the board bend down by just touching it, and readings of between three and a half and six pounds (1.5 and 2.75kg) were frequently recorded. To test the apparatus for malfunction, Crookes even went so far as to stand with his full weight on the table end of the board; but he could only exert a pound or two of pressure on it.

Having concluded his initial studies, Crookes's next plan was to return to the balance scale apparatus for even more stringent tests. He now wanted to isolate Home from the balance altogether, so he set about to develop a new device that would suit both his and Home's needs. This new apparatus was a little more complex than its predecessor, but it still basically represented only a modification of the mahogany board set-up. While he employed the same basic device, Crookes proceeded to place a vessel of water on the part of the board that had originally been bolted to the table. The idea was to have Home dip his hands into the water while trying to exert his psychokinesis onto the opposite end of the wood. Even with only this tenuous connection to the apparatus, Home was still able to display a great deal of PK. Crookes reported the following account of one of the experiments in the *Quarterly Journal of Science*:

> The apparatus having been properly adjusted before Mr Home entered the room, he was brought in, and asked to place his fingers in the water in the copper vessel ... He stood up and dipped the tips of his fingers of his right hand in the water, his other hand and feet being held. When he said he felt a power, force, or influence, proceding from his hand, I set the clock going, and almost immediately the end ... of the board was seen to descend slowly and remain down for about ten seconds; it then descended a little further, and afterwards rose to its normal height. It then descended again, rose suddenly, gradually sunk for seventeen seconds, and finally rose to its normal height, where it remained till the experiment was concluded. The lowest point marked on the glass was equivalent to a direct pull of about 5,000 grains.

Crookes was ultimately able to remove Home entirely from any contact with the scale. But he was still able to deflect the board even when standing three feet (1m) away from it.

The mediumship of Eusapia Palladino

Despite the scientific furor over D. D. Home and his phenomena prompted by Crookes's experiments, organized science still took little interest in the subject of psychokinesis. The reason was simple. Psychic phenomena contradicted the mechanistic-reductionist view of man that Victorian science was promoting. It was easier to ignore reports of PK than to confront them. When the scientific community was finally forced to evaluate evidence which suggested the existence of a psychic force, it reacted like an antibody warding off an infection. Crookes was branded a fool, an incompetent, and possibly even a co-conspirator in fraud.

The situation was hardly better fifteen years later in continental Europe. Yet it was at this time that some of the greatest scientific minds of Italy, Germany, France and Poland would join together to study PK when the next great subject came along. The critical year was 1888. The subject was a little Italian woman named Eusapia Palladino.

Despite the fact that Palladino eventually became the greatest medium of her day, we know relatively little about her background. She was born near Bari, Italy, in 1854 where her mother died in childbirth. Her father was murdered by thieves in 1866. Since raps and spontaneous telekinesis were observed in her presence even as a child, she was soon taken up by the Spiritualists who played an important part in her subsequent career. Soon she was giving private seances in Naples at the home where she was employed as a nursemaid.

Eusapia Palladino came to public attention in 1888 when Dr Ercole Chiaia, a well-known figure in Italy's psychic circles, published an open letter in a Rome newspaper on 9 August in which he challenged Cesare Lombroso — one of Italy's most prominent psychiatrists — to test Palladino for himself. Lombroso did, in fact, investigate Palladino and publicly reported his 'conversion' to psychical research in 1891.

The controversial Eusapia Palladino under test by the Society for Psychical Research, circa 1908. (Mary Evans/Society for Psychical Research)

As a result of Lombroso's enthusiastic report, a team of savants gathered in Milan to investigate the medium impartially in 1892. The composition of this commission was an ideal one. It included respected scientists and intellects of the day who were well aware of the problems they would be confronting as investigators. The committee members included, among others, Charles Richet, a physiologist from the Sorbonne, who would later receive a Nobel prize for his scientific work, and Carl du Prel, the noted philosopher. The commission supervised a lengthy series of sittings with Palladino, although the PK they witnessed was not great. It consisted mostly of touches and the curtains of the darkened seance room often billowed out mysteriously. They did, however, witness one of Palladino's more spectacular achievements — her partial materializations. Even when she was tightly held, phantom hands would materialize in the dark and touch and even caress the sitters. The commission was so impressed by these disembodied materialized hands which soared throughout the seance room that they concluded in their report that:

> It is impossible to count the number of times that a hand appeared and was touched by one of us. Suffice it to say that doubt was no longer possible. It was indeed a living, human hand which we saw and touched, while at the same time the bust and arms of the medium remained visible and her hands were held by those on either side of her.[12]

Professor Richet, however, left the seance with lingering doubts about what he had witnessed. He reported, quite apart from the committee's general conclusions, that:

> Absurd and unsatisfactory though they were, it seems to me very difficult to attribute the phenomena produced to deception — conscious or unconscious — or to a series of deception. Nevertheless, collective and indisputable proof that there was no fraud upon Eusapia's part, or illusion on our part, is wanting — we must therefore renew our efforts to obtain such proof.[12]

The Milan commission report encouraged scientists throughout Europe to study the Italian wonder. Professor Wagner, a zoology professor from St Petersburg, Russia, travelled to Naples to study her; she was shipped off to Poland for more tests; and Richet ultimately brought her to his private island off the coast of France for further observation.

The phenomena of Eusapia Palladino
Seances with Palladino usually presented a staggering array of phenomena.

So before continuing with a chronology of her career, I would like to give a fuller account of a typical seance. The following report is extracted from a sitting given by Palladino in France in the 1890s under the supervision of Camille Flammarion, the famous French astronomer mentioned in Chapter 1.[27] The seance began as everyone took their places around a table. A smaller table was set to one side of the room, while an area enclosed by curtains was constructed behind Palladino to serve as her cabinet.* Placed in the seance room but out of the medium's reach was a dish of putty, since earlier experimenters had found that Palladino would impress finger marks or even a mould of the side of a head in it from a distance. She could perform this feat even if she never came near the dish. The medium's hands and feet were held or controlled throughout:

> The candles are blown out, the lamp turned down, but the light is strong enough for us to see very distinctly everything that takes place in the salon. The round table which I had lifted and set aside, approaches the table and tries several times to climb up on it. I lean upon it, in order to keep it down, but I experience an elastic resistance and am unable to do so. The free edge of the round table places itself on the edge of the rectangular table, but hindered by its triangular foot, it does not succeed in clearing itself sufficiently to climb upon it. Since I am holding the medium I ascertain that she makes no effort of the kind that would be needed for this style of performance.
>
> The curtain swells out and approaches my face. It is at this moment that the medium falls into a trance.

But the seance was just getting going! Soon the psychic was producing materializations, i.e., quasi-material forms seemingly created out of some substance exuded from Palladino's body:

> I feel several touches on the back and on the side. M. de Fontenay receives a sharp slap on the back that everybody hears. A hand passes through my hair. The chair of M. de Fontenay is violently pulled, and a few moments afterwards he cries, 'I see the silhouette of a man passing between M. Flammarion and me, above the table, shutting out the red light.'
>
> This thing is repeated several times. I do not myself succeed in seeing this silhouette. I then propose to M. de Fontenay that I take his place, for, in that case, I should be likely to see it also. I soon distinctly perceive a dim

---

* A cabinet is an enclosed area used by a medium purportedly to generate psychic 'energy'. The utilization of a cabinet of one sort or another was a Spiritualist tradition of the day.

silhouette passing before the red lantern, but I do not recognize any precise form. It is only an opaque shadow (the profile of a man) which advances as far as the light and retires.

Later during the seance, Flammarion was able to witness ever more impressive psychokinesis:

The little round table, placed outside the cabinet, at the left of the medium, approaches the table, climbs clear up on it and lies across it. The guitar in the cabinet is heard moving about and giving out sounds. The curtain is puffed out, and the guitar is brought upon the table, resting upon the shoulder of M. de Fontenay. It is then laid upon the table, the large end toward the medium. Then it rises and moves over the heads of the company without touching them. It gives forth several sounds. The phenomena last about fifteen seconds. It can readily be seen that the guitar is floating in the air, and the reflection of the red lamp glides over its shining surface. A rather bright gleam, pear-shaped, is seen on the ceiling of the other corner of the room.

At this point in the sitting, Palladino requested a brief rest, during which the putty was placed on the table in front of her. The sitting then resumed, and further phenomena occurred:

The sitting is soon resumed as before, by the extremely feeble light of the red lantern . . . [Her spirit control] . . . is asked to continue his manifestations, and to show the impression of his head in the putty, as he has already several times done. Eusapia replies that it is a difficult thing and asks us not to think of it for a moment, but to go on speaking. These suggestions of hers are always disquieting, and we redouble our attention, though without speaking much. The medium pants, groans, writhes. The chair in the cabinet comes forward and places itself by the side of the medium, then it is lifted and placed upon the hands of M. Blech, at the other end of the table. Eusapia cries that she sees before her a head and a bust, and says 'E fatto' (it is done). We do not believe her, because M. Blech has not felt any pressure on the dish. Three violent blows as of a mallet are struck upon the table. The light is turned on, and a human profile is found imprinted in the putty. Mme Z. Bleck kisses Eusapia on both cheeks, for the purpose of finding out whether her face has not some odour (glazier's putty having a very strong odour of linseed oil, which remains for sometime upon one's fingers). She discovers nothing abnormal . . .

British and later European investigations

Such fantastic reports prompted Charles Richet to bring Palladino to his private island, Île Roubaud in 1894, in order to test her further. He was also hoping that officials from the Society for Psychical Research in Great Britain would join him and take part in the investigation. Even though the S.P.R. was then the most important investigative body in the world, the S.P.R. leaders had had trouble with fraudulent Spiritualist mediums in their home country. They were, therefore, extremely sceptical about the existence of psychokinesis and especially about Palladino. Nevertheless, two well-known English representatives from the S.P.R. — F. W. H. Myers and Sir Oliver Lodge — decided to cross the channel to join in the experiments with her. Both were impressed by what they were able to observe and shortly after invited the medium to England to be tested by other S.P.R. officials at Cambridge.

The Cambridge sittings of 1895 were the 'official' S.P.R. experiments with Eusapia Palladino, and many of the S.P.R. leaders took part in what would end up a total fiasco. The seances were held in semi-darkness as usual, while the medium's limbs were controlled by the investigators so that she could not cheat. Unfortunately, the British researchers were rather inept, and Palladino was able to size-up the situation easily. She started out-manoeuvring their control in order to use her hands and feet to fake her seance room wonders. Two of the sitters deliberately slackened their control to see if she *would* fake if and when given the opportunity, and Palladino took full advantage of the situation. She was easily detected in the fraud, so the investigators simply branded her a cheap fake and shipped her back to the Continent.

Researchers in Europe were dismayed by the S.P.R.'s conduct since they knew Palladino would cheat if given the chance. So they merely ignored the Cambridge affair and continued with new tests for her. Some of this work was extremely ingenious, since by the close of the Victorian era science was rapidly developing a new technology; and this technology was adopted in the study of Palladino. One experimenter found, for instance, that she could discharge an electroscope while standing a good distance away from it.

Another technological approach to Palladino's mediumship was the brain child of Professor Philippe Bottazzi.[11] Bottazzi was then the director of the Physiological Institute of the University of Naples, and his 1907 experiments were conducted in a laboratory room at his own university. He was interested in mechanically recording the results of Palladino's phenomena. So before each of his sittings, he attached devices to all the objects placed in the seance room which were, in turn, hooked to smoke paper cylinders. Therefore, whenever an object moved, a tracing would be made on the paper. Later he could then calculate how far and for what duration each of the objects had been moved during the seance. The tracings on the cylinders also revealed the amount of force used or required to move any specific object. As well as this, Bottazzi was able to encourage Palladino to display her powers in full light. These mini-experiments were usually conducted after a formal seance had been completed:

The light was slightly raised. M. Galeotti placed the letter-weight on the table and also the smoked cylinder, putting the pen in contact with the paper. I explained to Mme. Palladino what we wanted her to do; she was to lower the balance without touching it with her visible hands. The cylinder was put in motion and drew a horizontal line during several revolutions. A few seconds passed and then the curtain on the left advanced steadily toward the table, as if it was pushed by a hidden hand, the fingers of which were distinctly observable in relief against it; it seized the balance plate, pressed heavily on it, and then retired and disappeared. We stopped the cylinder, and we all verified the fact that the pen had inscribed a vertical line in the inked paper . . . whilst Palladino's hands were under our control!

Bottazzi calculated from the readings that the phantom hand had exerted 370 grams on the scale.

These and similar experiments were highly successful and interesting. But Bottazzi's own *personal* interest began to focus more and more on the medium's materialization phenomena, which often manifested during the formal sittings. The physiologist was able to examine several such forms during his sitting, and some of his observations of them are fascinating:

I felt an open hand seize me behind, gently, by the neck. Instinctively I let go of Dr Poso's right hand with my left and I carried it where I clearly felt this sensation of contact, and I found the hand which was touching me; a left hand, neither cold nor hot, with rough bony fingers which dissolved under pressure; they did not retire by producing a sensation of withdrawal, but they *dissolved*, 'dematerialised', melted.
   Shortly afterwards the same hand was laid on my head; I carried mine quickly to the spot, I felt it, I grasped it; it was *obliterated and again disappeared in my grasp*.
   Another time, later on, the same hand was placed on my right forearm without squeezing it. On this occasion I not only carried my left hand to the spot but I looked, so that I could see and feel at the same time; I saw a human hand, of natural colour, and I felt with mine the fingers and back

of a luke-warm hand, rough and nervous. *The hand dissolved and (I saw it with my eyes) retreated as if into Mme. Palladino's body, describing a curve.* I confess that I felt some doubt as to whether Eusapia's left hand had freed itself from my right hand, to reach my fore-arm; but at the same instant I was able to prove to myself that the doubt was groundless, because our two hands were still in contact in the ordinary way. If all the observed phenomena of the seven seances were to disappear from my memory, this one I could never forget! . . .

Two apparitions of human faces were also seen, not dark, but natural in colour, very pale, almost diaphanous, but well lit up. Each time the apparition was announced by Eusapia. This time a head appeared above hers; but I did not see it, and I report this according to what I was told by the others. It was asked: Who is it? And Eusapia replied in a thin voice, 'It is Peppino!' The second time Eusapia leaned her brow on mine and said immediately afterwards, 'Look!' We looked, and saw behind the edge of the left curtain a very pale human head clearly lit up.

With reports such as these emanating almost monthly from continental Europe, the S.P.R. was persuaded to work with Palladino once again. So in 1908 they sent a new committee to Italy to evaluate her. The team was well chosen. It consisted of Everard Feilding, one of the S.P.R.'s shrewdest investigators, and W. W. Baggally, who was an accomplished investigator and conjuror. Hereward Carrington, who had already written an encyclopaedic book on psychic fraud, completed the team. These three gentlemen had several things in common. They were all intensely devoted to the cause of psychical research, yet none of them had as yet encountered any genuine physical mediums. They were therefore very sceptical of Palladino and her claims. In fact, the S.P.R. specifically chose these researchers because they wanted this committee to be as tough and sceptical as possible. It is likely that the S.P.R. fully expected them to file a totally negative report. Before heading for Italy, the three researchers carefully evaluated all the earlier work that had been published on the medium, noting the strengths and weaknesses of such report. Then they planned well in advance the exact procedures they would use and how they would control the possibility of fraud.

The location of the experiments was a hotel room in Naples, especially rented for the tests. Despite the fact that they came well prepared for their task, the psychokinetic phenomena did not fail to occur. There were breezes, curtain billowings, telekinesis both in the dark and in the light, and some attempts at partial materialization. The S.P.R. investigators were so jolted by the experiences that they admitted in their final report that they had witnessed indisputable PK during the experiments.[12] Palladino had been vindicated, but the controversy about her abilities was to rage anew when Carrington brought her to the United States for further tests in November 1909.[14] These seances were a replay of the Cambridge fiasco, and Palladino returned ignominiously to Italy.[13] She died in 1918.

The mediumship of Stanislawa Tomczyk

It should not be thought that *all* the great physical mediums of the period worked in the dark. A few of them could produce PK displays in full light. Such was the case with a fascinating young woman from Poland, who was discovered in 1909. The investigator on the case was Dr Julien

Under Ochorowicz's close gaze, Stanislawa Tomczyk raises a pair of scissors, in Warsaw, 1909. (Mary Evans Picture Library)

Ochorowicz, a renowned psychologist of his day who headed the Institut Général Psychologique in Paris. The subject of his reports was Stanislawa Tomczyk, and the experiments were undertaken by Dr Ochorowicz at his home and the psychic's in Warsaw.[58]

Mlle Tomczyk was gifted with the ability to move and levitate small objects by PK. She could perform this feat by placing her hands on either side of the objects, but not touching them. The object would rise as she raised her hands and several photographs were taken of her demonstrations at extremely close range. Tomczyk could also deflect compass needles, and spontaneous apports (or teleportations) would often fall into the room during the experiments. These sessions were always carried out in full light.

Dr Ochorowicz initiated each experiment by first placing Mlle Tomczyk in trance, at which point a secondary personality of the psychic's, who called herself Little Stasia, would seemingly manifest. She, of course, claimed to be a spirit and the intelligence controlling the PK. The following is an extract from just one of Ochorowicz's experiments:

> A metallic support was plunged into a Leyden jar. Its lateral end carried a silk thread, which hung vertically and terminated a few inches lower in a very light tassel.
>
> When the jar was electrically charged, this little pendulum straightened out and receded from the bottle. By the side of this silk thread another thread twice as long is suspended, on the end of which a small metal bell is hung.
>
> The object was to put this bell into motion, by holding the hands immobile, placed on the table, on the two sides of the bell at a distance of about five inches.
>
> The medium gave me her hands to inspect and then placed them in an easy pose in the position indicated.
>
> After waiting several minutes, a certain oscillation of the bell was produced; but it was insufficient and the impatient medium preferred to do another experiment with the magic clock first of all.
>
> I consented: we made the experiment, which I will describe later and then returned to the bell.
>
> The 'current' being already formed, things went better now.
>
> The bell was shaken by an invisible force in different directions and rung several times, without the thread supporting it being much moved out of the perpendicular line.
>
> At the same time the tassel straightened itself, rose, but instead of going away from the Leyden jar, it drew near to it and held itself there, partly fell and then rose up again, keeping for some time an immobile position whilst the bell was feverishly shaken.

The movement of the tassel, quasi-attractive towards the jar, and quasi-repulsive in regard to the medium, was not desired by the latter, who had not noticed its existence, being solely occupied with the bell.

At all events, the current 'being developed', I said to the medium that I was going to place my hand between hers in order to see if I could feel anything. I put my hand close to her left hand, which remained immobile, *but I could not feel anything.* Mme M. S. (sensitive to the hypnoscope) did the same after me and she distinctly felt intense cold and some disagreeable pricking sensations at the end of the fingers.

But these attempts had an unpleasant sequence. The medium uttered a cry of pain, and showed me her right arm contracted and hyperaesthesised at the same time. I removed this state, not without some difficulty, and begged the medium to take a rest.

There were many enigmas about Mlle Tomczyk's curious form of mediumship. During her trances 'Little Stasia' would direct the phenomena and would seem to become a real intelligence, totally independent from the psychic's. Professor Ochorowicz at first considered Stasia only a secondary personality but later began to change his mind. His experiments with Tomczyk were full of surprises, and one of them came on January 17, 1909, when the psychologist was testing to see if his young subject could make a pendulum swing without touching it. Mlle Tomczyk could do this easily. But here is what happened when the researcher tried to do the tests again:

First of all we repeated the experiment of 'the mechanical action of the gaze'.
The large pendulum was certainly stopped mediumistically, then set going in the conditions of experiments 2 and 3. They were only more carefully observed. It took twenty minutes to effect the stoppage, which was almost sudden, leaving scarcely any oscillations even slight. It was the 'condensed, always invisible, hand' of little Stasia, which accomplished this *tour de force.*
A moment of rest; then the motion was effected more quickly and just as suddenly. At the end of two minutes, the pendulum regained its normal oscillations without hesitancy. The respiration of the medium, which was very carefully observed, did not come into play. The medium was not very fatigued, but, strange to say, I was much more fatigued than usual.
There was one curious detail this evening: At most of the previous seances, my two dogs took part as silent witnesses, a Newfoundland and a spaniel of mixed breed. Being well behaved they did not disturb us in any way but lay quietly on the floor near to an armchair about five yards from the couch, where the greater number of the experimenters [sic] took place.
At the moment when the medium declared that little Stasia had come

and seated herself in the armchair, the spaniel, who was lying facing the chair, growled. I turned round and saw the dog's gaze fixed on the armchair. The Newfoundland slept and paid no attention. He could not see the armchair; but the spaniel repeated his growl three times. He only calmed down when the medium declared that little Stasia was no longer there.

Tomczyk was, however, best known for her levitation performances, so Dr Ochorowicz focused intensely on these displays, often being able to examine the levitated objects at extremely close range. That is when he made an exciting discovery. The psychologist gradually began to see tiny spider-web like threads emanating from the medium's hands, which connected to the objects she was levitating. Now one could easily jump to the conclusion that these threads were merely strings. But this could hardly have been the case, since these threads had some very strange properties. Dr Ochorowicz reported that he could pass his hands through them, cut them, or do anything he liked to them. The rays would immediately resume their continuity when he was through disrupting them. As he wrote in one of his many reports on Mlle Tomczyk:

> I have felt these threads in my hand, on my face, on my hair. When the medium separates her hands the thread gets thinner and disappears; it gives the same sensation as a spider's web. If it is cut with scissors its continuity is immediately restored. It seems to be formed of points; it can be photographed and it is then seen to be much thinner than an ordinary thread. It starts from the fingers. Needless to remark that the hands of the medium were very carefully examined before every experiment . . .

Mlle Tomczyk could also levitate small objects enclosed in cups or funnels. She would move her hands alongside the shields, and the object inside the container would float up synchronously.

The results of the research
Despite the fierce controversies that surrounded the research on Eusapia Palladino and similar physical mediums, there were several beneficial outcomes. This research considerably advanced parapsychology's theoretical understanding of PK. Not only did it offer psychical research some of its best evidence for the existence of PK, it also succeeded in converting many brilliant minds to the cause of psychic studies. But even more importantly, probably for the first time in history, psychical researchers began wondering about the nature of the PK process and what mechanics lay behind it. There were two basic questions which

Palladino's investigators, in particular, kept asking themselves. They wanted to know what relationship existed between the psychic force and the medium's organism, but they also began wondering about the nature of the intelligence that manipulated the phenomena.

Several of the investigators did, in fact, adopt the spiritistic theory, believing therefore that Palladino was in contact with spirit agencies. But they were in the minority. Most of them assumed that her powers stemmed from some sort of force hidden within her body and controlled by her unconscious mind. Few of these researchers took Palladino's trance controls seriously, but considered them 'secondary' personalities capable of emerging from her mind. It is interesting, though, that these early parapsychologists conceptualized PK as basically a mysterious biological force and not necessarily a mental one. The fact that the medium's body would quiver and jerk sympathetically to the production of the PK was, to their minds, ample evidence for this theory. It is an idea that is being considered once more today, primarily by eastern European researchers who are positing the existence of a similar force. They have been calling it 'bioplasma', a subject we will be considering later.

Assessing the evidence

Physical mediumship is probably the most difficult area of PK research to evaluate because of its long association with fraud. Like so many poltergeist agents, physical mediums have an unfortunate propensity for 'helping out' their phenomena. The darkness of the seance room often serves as the cover for these clandestine manoeuvres. Despite the problems inherent in studying seance room PK, some of the performances of the great physical mediums of the golden age still seem impressive. D. D. Home — despite his long and varied career — was never caught in an act of fraud, and it is difficult to see how he could have successfully faked his fire-immunity, self-levitations, and many of his other feats. There were even instances during his career when the entire seance room would shake, and this became known as the 'earthquake' effect.

Eusapia Palladino, on the other hand, was prone to hoodwinking, but her methods of evading control were rather crude and well known to most of her experimenters. The fact that even those researchers who caught her in the act of fraud continued working with her undaunted is strong testimony to the impact she must have been able to make at times. The care with which the 1908 S.P.R. commission investigated her should make any student of the field think twice before dismissing the importance of her case. Similar comments could be applied to the case of Mlle Tomczyk and several other physical mediums of the day.

In short, the extant literature on physical mediumship is highlighted by some extremely impressive accounts. They have survived both the test of time and the piercing eyes of the sceptics.

4.
Rudi Schneider and Stella C.

Even though good physical mediums abounded in Europe before World War II, few of them ever cleared themselves from the dark cloud of fraud. Even if some of these psychics *could* produce genuine PK, they were virtually ignored by parapsychology if they had ever been charged — rightly or wrongly — with any wrong-doings. Despite this curious state of affairs, two cases that arose from this era of European psychical research were so striking that once again it almost looked as if organized science would take notice. Both cases were investigated and championed by Harry Price, a British ghost-hunter and entrepreneur of all things psychic, who maintained a laboratory in London.

Harry Price was a rather odd character. He was what we, today, might call a loner. He didn't get along with the leaders of the S.P.R., whom he considered biased and 'stuffy'. He also had a penchant for publicity and was constantly in the public eye promoting the cause of psychical research in any way he could. Since he lacked the formal education that S.P.R. leaders possessed, they in turn looked upon Price as an annoying *enfant terrible* liable to do more harm than good for the cause. Price's rather flamboyant personality did not endear him to these intellectuals either.

However, despite the many flaws in his personality, his knowledge of psychic studies was paralleled by few; he was one of the greatest authorities on fraud and conjuring; he was an able investigator; he operated one of the best psychic laboratories in Europe; and he was an ingenious inventor.

Price's background served him well; for while the S.P.R. maintained a cool indifference toward the study of physical mediumship, Price was actively recruiting some of the most talented mediums in Europe for his experiments during the 1920s. Almost single-handedly he kept the case for physical mediumship alive in England with his studies of two celebrated mediums — Stella Cranshaw and Rudi Schneider.

The discovery of Stella Cranshaw

Price met Stella Cranshaw by accident while commuting between London and his country home near Pulborough. One day in 1923, when he was taking his usual daily train ride home, he could not secure a compartment for himself, and found himself sharing one with a young woman. During the course of the trip, Price noticed that his companion had run out of reading material. So, always the perfect gentleman, he politely offered her his evening paper. The young woman declined the offer, but did ask to see a copy of Light, a Spiritualist periodical which Price was carrying. Price asked her if she had a particular interest in the psychic field. She answered by explaining that very strange things seemed to occur around her. Price's excitement grew as the lady described how spontaneous raps, cold breezes, and telekinesis had been plaguing her over the preceding few years. It did not take him long to recruit Stella C. (as she was called in his reports) for some controlled experiments. Stella was initially reluctant, but finally agreed to a short series of experiments.

The tests were run between March and September 1923 in Price's London laboratory.[65] He prepared himself and his lab for the tests carefully. For instance, since Stella claimed that she could produce 'cold breezes', Price placed thermometers in the seance room in such a way that they could be monitored by camera. This set-up would allow him to document scientifically any abnormal temperature fluctuations. He also set about inventing several gadgets with which to test Stella's PK; these included a special seance table that incorporated a fraud-proof chamber beneath it, in which were placed various target objects for the PK. This was a small table with a trap door cut into the top. The trap laid flat down, so it could not be opened from the top. It could only be opened by pushing it up from the underside of the table top. Price then placed wire gauze around the legs of the table, extending about half way to the floor. By placing another board under the table and connecting it to the gauze, the underside was completely sealed and formed a large compartment.

Price also developed what he called the 'telekinetoscope', which consisted of a bell-jar fixed to a metal base. Inside the jar was placed a telegraph-type key which, when depressed, would signal the experimenters by setting off a light or bell. The key was protected by a bubble blown around it. Tiny holes were drilled in the base unit. To

Harry Price, in the 1920s, wearing the 'mittens' and 'overshoes' he devised to give instrumental rather than human control over subjects' movements. (Mary Evans/Harry Price Collection, University of London)

activate the scope, the PK force would have to enter the jar, go through
the bubble without popping it, and then generate enough force to depress
the key. It was impossible to activate the scope in any other way.

The seances of Stella C.
Price conducted a series of thirteen seances with Stella C. They were
all held in dim light, although the experimenters were able to observe
everything quite distinctly. The first seance was held on 22 March, 1923,
but the phenomena were meagre. Stella did not go into trance, but was
nonetheless able to produce three full table levitations.

Price's third seance with Stella C. on 5 April produced the most
spectacular PK. While the seance table had been levitated on previous
occasions, Stella's psychokinesis thoroughly demolished it at this one.
Price described the incident in his book *Stella C*:

> The sitters and medium having formed themselves into a circle around the
> table with only the tips of their fingers touching the table top, great power
> was quickly developed, and movements of the table rapidly followed. The
> table was then completely levitated several times, remaining in the air for
> several seconds upon each occasion. Once the table rose completely above
> the heads of the sitters, some of whom had to rise in order to keep contact
> with it. During this levitation, the lower platform of the table struck the chin
> of Mr Price (who had remained seated, and had lost contact), and came
> to rest on his chest. The sitters then removed their hands from the table,
> only the finger-tips of the medium remaining upon it. Movements of the
> table still continued. The sitters again placed their fingers on the table top,
> when still further power was developed with increasing violence, two of
> the legs breaking away from the table with a percussion-like noise as the
> fracture occurred. At this juncture Mr Pugh excused himself and the seance
> continued without him. Colonel Hardwick, Mrs Pratt, and Mr Price still
> retained their fingers upon the top of the table, which was resting on the
> remaining leg. Suddenly, without warning, and with a violent snap, the table
> top broke into two pieces; at the same time the remaining leg and other
> supports of the table crumpled up, *the whole being reduced to what is little
> more than matchwood*. The sitting then concluded.
>
> The full red light was used throughout the sitting, except when a little
> daylight was allowed in the room. In the white light the table continued
> to move, but no levitation occurred. The medium became very sleepy during
> the latter portion of the sitting, and other sitters complained of exhaustion
> — but not to the same extent experienced at the last sitting. When the table
> top split in two, Mrs Pratt stated that she felt the 'force' run up the table,
> culminating at the top where the fracture occurred.

Stella Cranshaw, the non-professional medium, with whom Price had thirteen impressive seances in 1923. (Mary Evans/Harry Price Collection, University of London)

By the fourth seance, it was quite clear that Stella was entering a deep trance in order to facilitate the production of the PK. She even developed a 'spirit' control, and as the sittings proceeded her phenomena became bolder. Lights started appearing, the table would veer up and remain pivoted on two legs so securely that no one at the seance could push it back down, and masses of materialized matter would appear on the floor. On one occasion a large sprig of lilac, sixteen and a half inches (40cm) long, and in full bloom, fell into the locked seance room out of nowhere.

It was while the sittings were well in progress that Price introduced his trick devices. Stella's PK had no difficulty in moving toy musical instruments in the gauze cage under the trick table, playing upon them as well. The telekinetoscope was no challenge either, and her psychokinetic force activated the key with little difficulty.

Unfortunately, the Stella C. research progressed little from these initial studies, since she announced that she would not go on with the experiments after the first thirteen sessions. They were becoming tiring and were disrupting her life, she complained. Stella C. later gave another two sittings at Price's urgings, but then withdrew from psychical research altogether.

Even though Stella worked with only one committee of investigators, her brief career ranks as one of the most impressive cases of physical mediumship in the annals of psychical research. This is primarily because of the great care that went into the planning of the experiments. These sittings literally precluded fraud, and she succeeded at PK tasks which were totally impossible to fake.

The discovery of Rudi Schneider

The combined cases of Willi and Rudi Schneider of Braunau, Austria, also came to Price's attention during the 1920s.[66] Both brothers had shown evidence of remarkable psychokinetic abilities while still adolescents. Although they at first gave seances only for their family, both boys soon developed full physical mediumship as time passed. By 1922 the wondrous tales about young Willi's mediumship prompted Harry Price and Dr Eric Dingwall, then the S.P.R.'s research officer, to travel to Germany to test the older brother for themselves. Price was able to conclude after three sittings that:

> These seances were, to all intents and purposes, under our own control. We examined everything, affixed our own seals to the seance room door, etc., etc. After the seances Dingwall and I signed statements to the effect

Price with Willi Schneider in Austria, 1922. (Mary Evans/Harry Price Collection, University of London)

that we had witnessed genuine phenomena, which included many telekinetic movements — starting and stopping of a musical box in a gauze case — to order. The box also wound itself up. A pseudopod of handlike form picked up my handkerchief several times. Loud raps inside the cabinet were heard, the 'hand' or pseudopod showed itself against a luminous plaque, etc., etc. And all these phenomena occurred at a distance of some feet from the medium, who was controlled by two persons . . . Willi was searched and put into black tights, which were outlined with luminous bands and buttons. It was a wonderful display of phenomena, produced in really excellent red light.

Despite this glowing testimonial, Willi's mediumship did not escape suspicion. In 1924 he gave a series of sittings to the S.P.R. Little happened and the S.P.R. was markedly unimpressed. They tended to believe that since Willi usually gave seances at his family home, perhaps the only spirits present at his seances were the nimble hands of Papa Schneider.

Willi thereafter lost interest in his mediumship and retired from the psychic scene, devoting the rest of his life to dental work. In his place, his brother Rudi became a volunteer for experiment. Price had his first seance with Rudi in April 1926 and was impressed by the telekinesis, cool breezes, materialized hands, and the variety of raps he witnessed. Price's public endorsement of Rudi Schneider carried a great deal of weight, and Rudi's mediumship quickly became the centre of controversy in Europe. Some researchers considered him the best physical medium in Europe. Other investigators accused the whole Schneider family of working together to systematically defraud the investigators.

The fierce controversy ignited by Rudi's mediumship prompted several investigators to wonder if a fraud-proof experiment could ever be designed. The only type of control usually used was holding the medium's hands and feet, or outlining his body with luminous pins; but both systems of control had obvious pitfalls — especially since the physical mediums of this period invariably sat in the dark.

Finding a new method of control was just the type of challenge Price liked. By 1929 he felt that he had a fool-proof plan perfected, and he invited Rudi to his National Laboratory of Psychical Research to test it out. Rudi arrived in London late in 1929 and the experiments were soon underway.

For these important experiments, Price kept everyone in the seance room under *mechanical* control. Each of the sitters — as well as Rudi — were slipped into special gloves while their feet were placed on metal inductors. Circuits led from the gloves and the inductors to a display board consisting of several lights, each indicating one of the circuits. Neither Rudi nor any of the sitters could escape control after being hooked-up, since a signal light on the panel would go out if a circuit were broken. The investigators would then immediately know that someone had evaded control.

Despite these precautions, Rudi was able to produce a wide range of psychokinetic phenomena — there was the psychokinetic movement of objects, 'ectoplasic' masses appeared, the curtains in the seance room swung about, the seance table overturned, etc.

Further research with Rudi Schneider

The next triumph in Rudi's career came shortly after his London adventures. He underwent a subsequent number of ingenious tests at the Institut Métapsychique in Paris in November 1930.[60] These experiments were designed by Dr Eugene Osty, who was similarly preoccupied with finding a way to preclude any possibility of fraud. Osty and his son began their work by setting up a device in their laboratory's seance room that would project an infra-red beam. It was their hope to use the beam as a guard to separate Rudi from the objects his PK was supposed to manipulate during the experiments. The device was set up so that a camera would photograph Rudi if he evaded the experimenters' control and made a grab for the target objects — i.e., by penetrating the beam with his hand at the same time, he would be caught in *flagrante delicto* by the camera.

Dr Osty expected that Rudi would be able to move the seance objects without disrupting the beam. But the French physician was in for a surprise. During the course of several experiments, the camera kept flashing, thereby indicating that something had penetrated the beam. Yet the resulting photographs clearly showed that Rudi was safe in his chair with his hands still held by the investigators. Osty soon realized that somehow a force was leaving Rudi's body which, *while normally invisible to the eye, had enough substance to absorb about thirty per cent of the beam and set off the cameras.*

Taking a cue from his discovery, Osty proceeded to hook a bell device to the infra-red apparatus. His plan was to see how long Rudi's PK could penetrate the beam and ring the bell. Even though the medium's hands were continuously held by the experimenters, the bell would ring for periods up to and over one minute. Osty was spurred on even more by this new discovery; he decided to revise his set-up still further, so that a record could be made of the exact oscillations of the beam as

Rudi Schneider tested in London by Fraser Harris, 1932. (Mary Evans/Society
for Psychical Research)

Rudi's PK penetrated it. That is when he made his most famous and meaningful discovery. Rudi would always hyperventilate during his sittings, and the oscillations of the infra-red beam were always exactly double that of Rudi's respiration rate. This finding proved the existence of a tie-up between the PK and the medium's organism.

It was only after the Institut Métapsychique experiments were completed that Rudi's mediumship was first called into question. It was to become a blemish on an otherwise stainless career. Harry Price was able to secure Rudi's services for another series of seances at his laboratory in 1932. It was clear that by now Price was jealous of Osty's work, which was generating more interest than his own previous experiments. For this new series Price did away with his electrical circuits and controlled Rudi merely by holding his hands in the dark. The goal of the experiments was to photograph Rudi's materializations and telekinesis. Several sittings were held, many photographs were taken, and then Rudi went back to the Continent without any hint of the storm that was about to break back in London.

It was not until months later that Price announced that he had caught Rudi in fraud. He published one of the photographs taken during the 1932 series which clearly showed Rudi evading control.[67] The plate showed him freeing an arm to produce the manifestations. Rudi was enraged when he heard about the charge, and denied it with a mixture of anger and consternation. He realized that his mediumship was now in doubt, despite the rigorous care with which the earlier work had been executed; but the controversy was never resolved.

It wasn't until over forty years later that Rudi was vindicated. The plate showing the alleged fraud was discovered among Price's archives, deposited with the University of London. Several analyses of the plate suggested that it could have been a cleverly contrived composite, perhaps created by Price himself to 'get back' at Rudi for going over to Dr Osty and other researchers in England after that.

Assessing the evidence

The research with both Stella Cranshaw and Rudi Schneider brought a new experimental sophistication to the seance room. The psychical research of that era sought not only to implement fraud-proof conditions, but wanted to design fraud-proof tests as well. They apparently succeeded on both counts. The discoveries made during these years also took our understanding of the PK process further away from the spiritualistic milieu, and aimed it more towards the study of human biology.

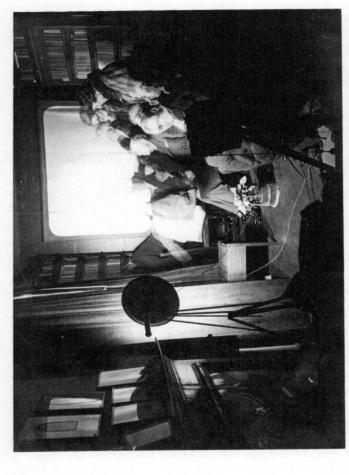

This photograph of 3 March 1932 shows, according to Price, Rudi Schneider
in the act of cheating. However, some critics claim that the picture is itself a cheat contrived by Price to discredit Rudi.
(Mary Evans/Harry Price Collection, University of London)

5.

Modern PK Breakthroughs

Great care went into the research conducted with such physical mediums as Palladino, Rudi Schneider, Stella C. and Stanislawa Tomczyk. Despite the results of these investigations, the whole practice of physical mediumship began to die out after the 1930s. Researchers looked in vain to find comparable psychics who could take their places. None emerged. The reason for this decline was probably because Spiritualism — which gave rise to and encouraged new and promising physical mediums — went into a decline itself during these years. The milieu that gave rise to the great mediums simply dissolved, while most psychical researchers began looking more and more toward statistical research to prove the case for psychic phenomena.

When the great physical mediums began to disappear, parapsychologists simply stopped looking for them. They were also too wary of the ever-present possibility of fraud to care when sensational reports did occasionally come to their attention. Researchers became so disenchanted with this whole area of research that by the 1940s and '50s, many of them were openly questioning whether such strong PK ever really existed. The answer was to come in the 1960s, from far behind the Iron Curtain.

The discovery of Nina Kulagina

Mrs Nina Kulagina may look just like a typical Russian housewife, but she is probably the most celebrated PK subject in the world today. Not only have scientists in the Soviet Union been studying her for several years, but scientists around the world have ventured behind the Iron

Curtain to observe her demonstrations. They have watched her slide objects across table tops, gyrate suspended ping-pong balls in plexiglass cubes, create burn marks by merely touching an onlooker's arm and many other psychic feats.

Nina Kulagina (whose maiden name of Nelya Mikhailova is sometimes used in material published on her) was born in 1928. She survived the agony of the German seige on Leningrad, having herself borne arms against the invaders as a teenager. By the end of the war she had been promoted to senior sergeant. She eventually married, had three children, and now has grandchildren. But, until only recently, Kulagina has been devoting most of her time to scientific experimentation in hopes of learning more about her psychokinetic abilities.

Just how Kulagina discovered her PK capabilities is a bit puzzling since the psychic herself has offered us contradictory accounts of the story. The most reliable version is that she accidentally developed PK while undergoing testing at the Institute of Brain Research in Leningrad where L. L. Vasiliev — the dean of Soviet parapsychology — was testing people to see if they could tell colours by touch. While working with Kulagina in the early 1960s, he noticed that small objects sometimes moved under her fingertips. This exciting observation led him to test the woman for PK powers, by seeing if she could deflect a compass. Later he encouraged her to develop her abilities further.[44]

Early research and documentations

That Soviet parapsychologists had discovered a remarkable PK subject only became known to the West several years after Kulagina began her PK work with Vasiliev, who died in 1966. Western scientists first began taking an interest in the Russian psychic in the late 1960s, when films of her PK began to show up in Europe; some of these films had been smuggled out of the Soviet Union. They first made their appearance in England and came to the attention of Mr Benson Herbert, a physicist by training, who has his own private laboratory in Downton, Wiltshire. He began publishing translations of Soviet papers on Kulagina in his own *Journal of Paraphysics* in the 1960s and also succeeded in making the first detailed analysis of the Kulagina films.

One of the films that Herbert was able to procure was taken by Dr Zdenek Rejdak, a Czech scientist at the Prague Military Institute who has been actively engaged in parapsychological work for several years. Rejdak visited Kulagina in Leningrad in 1968 to test her and photograph the PK. The tests only began after he had searched her for concealed magnets or strings:

After we sat down around the table I required Mrs Kulagina to leave the position at which she had decided to sit, and to sit at the opposite side of the table. The first test was to endeavor to turn a compass needle first to the right and then to the left. Mrs Kulagina held her hands approximately 5-10 cm over the compass during the experiment, as well as during the following ones. After an interval of concentration, the compass-needle turned more than ten times. Thereafter, the entire compass-needle turned on the table, then a matchbox, some separate matches, and a group of about 20 matches at once.

I placed my gold ring on the table; it moved faster than all the other objects . . . I chose some glass and china objects from the buffet, weighing from 10 to 20 dg., and Mrs Kulagina made them move as well. On request, she could induce motion in the objects, while they were on a seat or on the floor. All this was performed in full light. The gold ring which she had made move was taken by me from my finger and put on the table. She passed her hands over it and the ring moved toward her. Threads or other attachments were out of the question.

The matches we used had not been examined because they belonged to us, as also did the match-box, and so could not have been prepared by her. Fraud was impossible, as she was sitting in a fully illuminated room controlled by Professor Sergeyev, Dr Zvenev, Mr Blazek, and myself. Other objects . . . were selected by myself and so she had no opportunity of preparing them.

We asked her to make the matches move not only toward her but also away from her. We also asked her to move only one match, specified by us, from the whole group of matches. Later we put two compasses before her and asked her to move any one of them. All these tasks were fulfilled. It appears therefore that the exteriorized energy can be directed by the subject's will. [68]

During this entire series of tests, Kulagina's body was being monitored psychophysiologically. When the experiments were completed, it was clear that she had lost weight; her heart was beating erratically; her blood-sugar had increased; and her muscles ached. This would tend to indicate that Kulagina undergoes a great deal of stress during the production of her PK.

Mme Kulagina's reactions to her PK are in fact very similar to the ones about which Palladino would complain at the end of one of her seances. She too was severely affected after the completion of a trying set of tests. She lost weight, cramped up, and would even vomit. This would indicate that both Kulagina and Palladino exercised very similar powers, although the tendency was to express themselves differently. Kulagina had little need for the seance room trappings that Palladino had deemed necessary.

The films made and collected by Dr Redak and his colleagues are fascinating. They were publicly shown in England to members of the Society for Psychical Research on March 14, 1968, and caused no little sensation.[34-6] The films depicted several astonishing (purported) demonstrations of PK. For example, small objects were seen to move after being placed in a transparent box. Another sequence showed Kulagina moving a cigarette balanced on end without toppling it over. The *pièce de résistance*, however, showed an experimenter balancing a cigar case on the top of a playing card, both of which are then placed in a box. Kulagina can be seen to concentrate and the card with the case slide across the box together — the case remaining upright at all times.[69]

The films did confirm written reports about Kulagina's powers, which were then becoming more available from Soviet sources. One of these reports was written by Leo Kolodny, who published it in *Pravda* in March 1968.[48]

Kolodny visited Kulagina at her Leningrad apartment personally to observe her PK. The two of them sat together before a table and the writer began by placing his own fountain pen cap along with a glass on the table. Kulagina was soon focusing her firm gaze on the targets, willing them to move with all her might; but nothing seemed to be happening. Kolodny was writing some hurried notes for his article at the time and was not paying attention to what Kulagina was doing, but on glancing up:

> . . . I write and at the same time I glance at the cap. I write until the pen drops from my hand in amazement; the cap creeps along the table cloth. At first it makes a sharp jerk, another jerk, and crawls toward the very edge of the table. Behind it crawls the neighboring tumbler, as if they are hauled in one and the same harness . . .

In order to test the psychic further, Kolodny (who admitted that by this time he had a 'lump stuck in my throat') placed the glass over the pen cap. The little cap acted like a trapped insect. It meandered back and forth under the barrier, bumping into the glass walls from side to side. The next day Kolodny returned and filmed the PK.

Not all of the experiments undertaken with Kulagina, however, have been conducted by newswriters, since Soviet scientists have studied her as well. Chief among these has been Dr Genady Sergeyev of the A. A.

Utkomskii Physiological Institute, a military facility in Leningrad. He discovered that Kulagina's body radiates electromagnetic currents when she is performing her PK. Much of this radiation, Sergeyev claims, is generated from the back of her head.

Soviet scientists have also discovered several other factors which contribute to, or seem to guide, Kulagina's psychokinesis. They have learned that a friendly and informal atmosphere helps her. New tests seem to take more 'energy' out of her, and she has to rest frequently during them. On the other hand, she can manipulate material no matter what it is made from. They have found that her PK can be used on metals, plastics, fabrics, and organic materials. Even the very movements of the PK-affected objects appear to be governed by a few rigid principles. For example, Soviet researchers have discerned that:

(1) It is easier for Kulagina to roll objects such as cigarette or cigar containers than to shift them from an upright position.

(2) When Kulagina is working with new objects, they always move away from her. Only after practice can she attract them.

(3) However, those objects that are being attracted to the psychic's body move faster and more energetically.

(4) It takes greater energy for Kulagina to move objects further away from her than ones which are close at hand.

(5) Often the objects begin their motion as though imitating the psychic's own bodily movements. When she swings and contorts her body as she strains to exert the PK, the objects will often move in similar fashion.

(6) Even after a test is over, an object might continue to move even though Kulagina is no longer attempting to influence it.

Soviet scientists have also studied how screening affects the objects that Kulagina tries to influence by PK. They have found that screening the target objects with lead-impregnated glass, paper, metal plates, wood and so forth has no affect on the PK. Shielding will not affect it even if a screen is imposed around the objects *while* they are in motion. Kulagina's only limitation is that she cannot move objects placed in a vacuum.[47]

The investigations of J. G. Pratt

With provocative reports such as these coming out of Soviet bloc nations, it was not long before Western scientists began travelling to the Soviet Union to see Kulagina for themselves. One of the first American parapsychologists to make the journey was Dr J. Gaither Pratt from the

University of Virginia's parapsychology division. Pratt first heard about Kulagina during a symposium on parapsychology which he attended in the Soviet Union in June 1968. Not only did he hear the reports about her at that time, but he saw some of the films of her demonstrations.

It took Pratt two years to get back to Russia, but he finally arrived in Leningrad in June 1970, accompanied by Dr Jurgen Keil, a psychologist from the University of Tasmania. Unfortunately, Pratt was only able to confer with Soviet scientists working with Kulagina on this trip and did not get to see her for himself. He therefore made a return visit that September along with Champe Ransom, another researcher from the University of Virginia. His first tests took place in his own hotel room. [64]

The first test was designed to see whether Kulagina could influence photographic film merely by concentrating on it, since some evidence exists that she can 'fog' it by PK. Pratt had brought along an old Polaroid camera, but Kulagina failed to impress anything on the film. Pratt and Ransom then turned to testing her psychokinesis, by asking her to slide some small objects across a table in the room. Then they left the room in order, they said, to give Kulagina a chance to warm up; and the psychic had no idea that she was actually being secretly watched from a hallway. Pratt later wrote that:

> ... I could see Kulagina through the open door. She was sitting on the far side of a small round table facing me and the matchbox and compass were lying in front of her on the table. After a time I noticed that the matchbox, while she held her hands stretched out toward it and appeared to be concentrating very hard, moved several inches across the table in her direction. She put the box back near the centre of the table and it moved again in the same way. [64]

Champe Ransom took over Pratt's vantage point and he too watched the matchbox move. It approached the compass, which also rested on the table, and the two objects began to move jointly. Later that day they witnessed further inexplicable object-movements.

Pratt and Keil paid yet another visit to the Soviet Union in February 1971, but this trip was to be a disappointment. From what Pratt was later able to surmise, Soviet officials had heard a review of the recently published *Psychic Discoveries Behind the Iron Curtain*, a rather sensationalist and factually inaccurate book that was fast becoming a bestseller in the United States. [59] Offended by the claims made in the book, they had placed Kulagina strictly off-limits to foreign investigators.

But Pratt was persistent and he and Keil paid one further visit to the Soviet Union in September 1971. When they arrived in Leningrad they immediately contacted Kulagina. They really only expected to pay the celebrated psychic a social visit, but that evening Kulagina gave them a private performance *par excellence*. She was able to move several objects for the visitors, even though she had not given any demonstrations for a year. The most striking thing about these impromptu experiments was that Kulagina did not seem to have very much control over her PK. Pratt and Keil would place objects on a table for her to move, and she would end up moving one article while consciously focusing on a different one.

Further independent investigations

Pratt and Keil's investigations were basically meant to be observational. None of their tests were in any way designed to discover anything novel about Kulagina's powers. Consequently their tests tell us very little about the nature of the PK process. One Western scientist who *has* studied Kulagina in order to explore the mechanics and range of her abilities, however, is Benson Herbert.

Herbert visited the Soviet Union in July 1972, along with his associate Manfred Cassirer, to attend meetings with Soviet colleagues and to learn about any advances they were making in their PK research. This trip also enabled them to work directly with Kulagina. Herbert, Cassirer, and Kulagina all met together for the tests at a Leningrad hotel. Unfortunately, Kulagina was not in any mood to offer a demonstration that evening. She was prostrated by a heat wave which was engulfing the city, and had been ill the day before. The skies were threatening a thunderstorm and she explained that she did not like performing when the atmosphere was electrified. The visit was not a complete failure though, for before leaving Kulagina was able to demonstrate one of her more peculiar phenomena. Herbert was later to write:

> Kulagina gripped my left arm about two inches above the wrist — in this tropical heat wave my shirt sleeves were rolled up — and I waited, not quite knowing what to expect. If anything, I thought I may feel some beneficial or soothing influence, but for two minutes, I felt nothing whatever, save only a natural increase of warmth under her hands. Then, quite abruptly, I experienced a new sensation, which I described at the time as a kind of 'heat' but which now, after much reflection, I believe to be more akin to a mild electric shock.
>
> It was however enough to be quite unpleasant; my arm writhed and my

Nina Kulagina, photographed by Manfred Cassirer during his visit to the Soviet Union in July 1972. (Mary Evans Picture Library)

face grimaced, to the amusement of the onlookers. After perhaps two minutes, I came to the conclusion that I could not endure the sensation a moment longer, and disengaged my arm from Kulagina's formidable handclasp. One interesting feature was that throughout these two minutes, the sensation as far as I could judge remained quite constant; and it began suddenly as if with the turning on of a switch. There was no gradual build-up of sensation and discomfort such as might have been expected through someone gripping one's arm too tightly.[37]

Kulagina attempted to replicate the demonstration on Cassirer's arm, but failed. Then she turned her almost sadistic attention on the investigators' translator. She gripped the translator's arm and soon her new victim was grimacing with pain.

Herbert was able to make a more detailed study of Kulagina's PK in April 1973 at the Hotel d'Europe in Leningrad. This was his second trip to the USSR to see the psychic, and for these tests he brought several devices with which he hoped to measure her PK. One of them was a floating hydrometer.* Herbert hoped that Kulagina could influence the device while it was placed in a saline solution and protected by an earthed screen and an electrostatic probe. The physicist could then calculate the amount of force Kulagina had exerted from the readings.

When Kulagina finally arrived for the tests, along with Dr Sergeyev, Herbert believed he would be disappointed. She had been ill again and it momentarily looked as if the tests would be a wash-out. But even Herbert was not ready for what was to come:

Presently, Kulagina began to look around the room, and the floating hydrometer caught her eye. It seemed to fascinate her and she asked its purpose. I explained the functioning of the apparatus, and Professor Sergeyev stated that my electrostatic probe was very similar to a device he himself had invented some years previously.

Suddenly Kulagina startled us by walking over to the table and placing her hands in various positions near the rim of the metal cylinder (6 inches in diameter, 5 inches high) that encased the glass vessel in which floated the hydrometer. At her sudden decision to overcome her indisposition and make an attempt at a demonstration, we were electrified into activity. I hastily switched on the equipment and all of us formed a circle around the table, with a battery of cameras poised.

* A hydrometer is a tubular device that scales the gravity or density of any liquid in which it sits by the level to which it sinks.

As her hand approached the probe, I noticed with surprise that she evidenced much less electrostatic activity than I had expected (later we found that the field strength surrounding her body was only about three-quarters that surrounding the others present, at equal distances.) The hydrometer began to move slowly through the saline solution. This movement was repeated several times. However, her hands sometimes contacted the apparatus, and I thought it likely that the motion was due to vibration, but later all of us tried for the same effect, without success. Then Kulagina returned to her chair, three to four feet from the apparatus, and sat down as if exhausted.[41]

Even though she was now quite a distance from the device, she was still fascinated by it:

Suddenly we fell silent, having noticed that Kulagina, after moving her chair only a few inches nearer to the table, had apparently fallen into a state of concentration (not, I think, a trance), and was gazing intently at the hydrometer. Kulagina slowly moved her arms, raising them so that the palms of the hands faced toward the instrument. Shortly after, the hydrometer began to move away from her in a straight line across the full diameter of the vessel, a distance of 2½ inches and came to rest at the opposite side, the transit occupying some 90 seconds. She then lowered her arms and remained quite still. The hydrometer remained stationary for two minutes, then commenced to move again, at the same speed as before, retracing its path until stopped by the edge of the glass nearest to her.

Kulagina capped her demonstration by making a compass deflect in short, jagged movements. She then demonstrated the 'psychic burn' phenomenon that she had shown Herbert on the occasion of his last visit. She grasped the physicist's arm, and the pain was soon so intense that he began clenching his fist and stamping his foot on the ground. Herbert later explained that he could only take the agony for about five minutes before he had to ask Kulagina to stop. A reddish burn mark soon developed at the point where Kulagina had gripped his arm.

The current status of research on Nina Kulagina
There is little information at present about recent research on Nina Kulagina's psychokinesis. Some reports came out a few years ago which claimed that her whole system was being torn apart by her demonstrations, but it is difficult to determine the truth or fiction of these claims. It seems well-documented that her blood sugar level, portions of her brain, and several of her internal organs are adversely

affected during the course of her displays. But whether or not Kulagina is literally 'tearing herself apart' by her constant PK demonstrations is a debatable point.

There are, in fact, so many different aspects to Kulagina's PK that it is hard to do justice to her in this chapter. Back in 1976, however, several researchers — including Dr Jurgen Keil, Benson Herbert, Dr J. G. Pratt, and Dr Montague Ullman — analysed all the studies published on her to date and issued a joint report on her powers.[44] By re-analysing all this literature the four parapsychologists felt that some definite statements could be made about the process behind the Soviet housewife's psychokinetic powers:

(1) Many of the early tests showing the paranormal movement of small objects were carried out in a manner which seems to have excluded the possibility of fraud.

(2) Objects will often move even after Kulagina has ended one of her demonstrations.

(3) Objects often move in circular trajectories as well as toward and away from her.

(4) Sometimes items other than the specifically designated target will be affected by the PK and will be inadvertently moved.

(5) More than one object will sometimes move when Kulagina is demonstrating her PK, but they all usually move in a uniform direction.

(6) Kulagina can on occasion move a group of objects simultaneously in several different directions.

(7) She can use PK to disturb the movements of an object already in motion, and can even make such an object change direction.

(8) She can exert her PK on living material, such as by slowing down and stopping a frog's heart.

(9) There is some evidence that Kulagina discharges energy from her head while concentrating.

(10) There is no evidence that electrical fields come into play during her performances.

(11) Screening has little appreciable affect on Kulagina's PK.

(12) Storms tend to inhibit it however.

(13) Kulagina loses weight during her PK exhibitions and shows other signs of physical stress.

Latest word has it that Kulagina has decided not to return to the scientific laboratory, although she still occasionally gives demonstrations. She is growing older now, and the experiments are becoming too much of a strain upon her.

Despite the fact that Nina Kulagina is probably the most provocative PK subject being studied today, she certainly has her imitators. Ever since she became the centre of international attention, more and more subjects have begun to appear on the psychic scene claiming similar abilities. Many of these psychics, or self-proclaimed sensitives, have also come out of the Soviet bloc nations.

The electrostatic PK abilities of Alla Vinogradova

One of these gifted subjects is a young educational psychologist named Alla Vinogradova, currently living in Moscow. Vinogradova comes from a scientific family and her husband is Dr Victor Adamenko, a talented young Soviet physicist who has done much to spearhead Soviet parapsychology. Vinogradova first became intrigued with the possibilities of psychokinesis through watching films of Kulagina in action. Soon she began practising too, imitating the older woman. Eventually she became rather proficient at producing a weak semblance of Kulagina's displays, and soon learned to make small cylinders roll under her hands as she swayed back and forth. There is, however, considerable debate currently going on within parapsychological circles whether or not she has been able to develop genuine PK abilities or has just learned some curious method of manipulating electrostatic forces. If the latter is the true explanation for her abilities, then she is really not a psychic subject at all.

Alla Vinogradova was introduced to the parapsychological community at large during an international psychology congress that convened in Tokyo, Japan, in August 1972. Victor Adamenko was present at the meeting and publicly showed films of his wife's PK as he made his formal presentation about her. The films show Vinogradova seated before a dielectric table with a paper cylinder in front of her. She can be seen rolling her hand above the object, and it, too, rolls as if connected to her hand by an invisible string. Other segments showed her hand repulsing the movement of the cylinder, the way concordant poles of two magnets will repel one another.[1]

Despite the clarity of the films, just what they are showing has become a matter of debate. A somewhat critical review of them was published in the September/October 1972 issue of the *Parapsychology Review* by Benson Herbert.[39] He aptly points out that Vinogradova's demonstrations are not unequivocally displays of PK, since the same effects can be produced by just about anyone charged with static electricity and standing on an insulated mat. He points out, a bit humorously, that wearing fashionable synthetic underwear would even produce such a charge, since the friction between the skin and the material is enough to produce it!

Despite these reservations, many features of Vinogradova's demonstrations seem to defy the notion that they are *simply* the result of static charges. For instance, a human hand charged with static electricity will usually only *attract* foreign objects. Vinogradova can, however, clearly repel them as well. She can also produce an enormously high voltage gradient and seems to possess extraordinary control over the field she is creating, whatever its nature may be. This does not sound very much like normal static electricity. Note, too, that she can selectively manipulate this force, and can, among other things, move one of two objects placed side by side. She can also produce her effects while standing barefoot on a metal floor while wearing a grounded metal bracelet. These guards should be able to ground any normal electrical build-up that the subject might be generating.

One witness who believes that the mystery behind Vinogradova's powers is far from understood is Pamela Painter de Maigret, an American writer who visited the Adamenkos in Moscow in 1973. There she watched the controversial psychologist move cylinders back and forth across a table top. It took immense effort and strain for Vinogradova to produce the effects, but once she was 'warmed up' she could move the objects with ease. To quote from de Maigret's account of the meeting:

> [The cigar tube] . . . rocked back and forth several times, then slowly began to roll across the plastic table top away from her hand.
> When the cylinder neared the outer edge, Alla quickly reached over the table and put her hand on the far side to it. It stopped abruptly six or eight inches from her hand, rocked a few times and then started to roll in the opposite direction. Alla's hand was always at least half a foot away from both the table and the cylinder. She continued while the tube rolled across the table several times. Each pass seemed to become easier for her. The strain and tension left her face; her body became more relaxed; the cylinder moved with greater ease . . . [52]

Mrs de Maigret was in for a surprise, though, when Vinogradova stepped up to her and suggested that *she* herself could roll the cigar tube. Vinogradova took the writer's hands and rubbed them briskly. Then, hand in hand, they jointly pushed the tube back and forth. 'I thought

I could feel a faint repulsive energy between the cylinder and my hands,' writes Mrs de Maigret, 'it was rather like the feeling of trying to force similar poles of two magnets together.' Of course, what Mrs de Maigret has really given us is a perfect description of what a static charge feels like.

After Vinogradova finished 'helping' her out, Mrs de Maigret discovered that she could produce the movements independently. Her power soon petered out, so Vinogradova had to re-charge her, and immediately Mrs de Maigret found her quasi-PK ability reborn!

Not all of Vinogradova's demonstrations can be easily explained as some sort of electrostatic-field manipulation, though. Some of her powers smack of genuine psychokinesis. For example, Mrs de Maigret reports one incident that seems more in line with psychokinesis than with a simple electrostatic discharge:

> At the end of the afternoon's filming I asked Alla if she could move other objects too. She said, 'Of course,' so the group of us hunted about in our pockets and came up with a metal pen cap, an all-plastic pen cap, a Ping-Pong ball, various coins, some wooden matches and the small cardboard box they came in. We pushed the Plexiglas cube toward a corner so the crew could remove their equipment, and we all crowded around to see Alla give an informal demonstration.
>
> I noticed that although Alla moved them all with facility, the various objects differed in the ways they moved. She could roll the pen caps in bumpy fashion due to their pocket clips or could make them skip without rolling. She could push them over from a standing position but could not raise them upright from a prone position. The Ping-Pong ball could be made to skid across the table or to roll or bounce. To bounce it Alla quickly raised and lowered her hand about six inches above the ball. The ball started to shake, then bounced a bit and with each bounce went higher. This was the only time I saw Alla appear to draw something toward her hand rather than push it away.
>
> The matches, which were emptied out of their box in a jumbled heap on the table, reacted in even stranger fashion. At first the jumbled mass did not move as a whole. As Alla pushed at them from about a foot away individual matches suddenly jumped, scattering the other matches around them. A momentum appeared to be building up that reminded me of popcorn held over a fire. The wooden matches 'popped' in all directions. Only after several minutes did Alla get the whole mass to move away from her across the table; individual matches still popped around. I thought that chemicals in the match heads might have affected the movement but when we snapped the heads off a dozen or so they still reacted in the same way.[52]

The strange powers of Alla Vinogradova remain a mystery at the present time since it is possible to offer several arguments both for and against the possibility that they are paranormal. But there is another possibility we must consider as well: could it be that Vinogradova at first discharges an electrostatic field which then gradually, or sporadically, changes to psychokinesis?

This is a theory that some people might find attractive. It also suggests that PK may have some peculiar link with electricity, and would be consistent with the fact that Eusapia Palladino could, for instance, discharge an electroscope. (Nina Kulagina, on the other hand, actually produces sparks from her hand while generating her PK effects.) Even in many poltergeist cases, the force may begin by disrupting electrical equipment before going on to more conventional object-throwing. It is unfortunate that the possible relationship between PK and electricity has not been explored by parapsychologists since Alla Vinogradova may have the peculiar ability to manipulate electrostatic fields *through* small amounts of PK. The static charge may serve as some sort of carrier.

The controversial case of Dr Julius Krmessky

Another subject of some interest living in eastern Europe is Dr Julius Krmessky, a Czech physicist who was at one time a lecturer at the State Pedagogical Institute in Bratislava. Dr Krmessky believes that he has discovered a whole new energy form which can be moulded by the will. He came to this conclusion when he discovered that he could gyrate little paper mobiles, hung by threads or balanced on pins, merely by bringing his hand close to them. While Krmessky is very intrigued by the possibility that these effects are caused by some form of new energy, there are, however, many normal factors that can account for the movements. Heat generated by his hands as well as tiny wind currents and static electricity can all feasibly account for these movements, and there is little evidence that he had ever controlled for these possibilities while testing himself. Dr Krmessky's talents may be very similar to Alla Vinogradova's in one respect, though. It is possible that genuine psychokinesis will, on occasion, interplay with the normal forces which usually affect these mobiles.

Benson Herbert visited Krmessky in October 1971 and witnessed several performances given by the physicist at his lab. Herbert soon realized that what he was seeing was hardly evidence of PK or for a new energy. So Krmessky, at Herbert's insistence, participated in another series of tests in which the target objects were shielded. Some of these demonstrations were more impressive. Herbert later reported that:

... in some experiments under total shielding conditions, the systems certainly appear to obey Dr Krmessky's commands . . . Thus, a vane, floating upon water in a wine glass and completely covered by a glass vessel, remained quite stationary for ten minutes; then Dr Krmessky began his experiments. He started with quiet concentration on the vane from a distance of four feet; no one moved; doors and windows remained shut. Within four minutes, the vane was rotated $45°$ in the desired direction, then a further $90°$, only coming to rest when Dr Krmessky retired to an armchair about ten feet away, and ceased to look at the vane. This struck me as either paranormal or an improbable coincidence.[38]

During this same series of tests, Herbert watched as Krmessky moved a paper cylinder resting on a needle point and shielded inside a tin can. Despite these impressive displays, it is still very hard to determine whether the 'Krmessky-effect' is genuinely paranormal.

I was finally able to watch a film in 1974 showing Dr Krmessky in action. The segment was one of a number of film clips that two writers of my acquaintance had obtained from their east European contacts. I wasn't very impressed by what I saw. The target object for the filmed demonstration was a paper vane balanced on a base and placed at the end of a table. Dr Krmessky can be seen seated at the opposite end of the same table, staring at it. The paper begins to revolve in little spurts of movement while he concentrates on it. The vane's motions rather reminded me of how objects moved by Kulagina will also slide in a sort of 'stop-start' spurting action. Since Dr Krmessky was seated about five feet or so from the target, it is hard to see how static or air currents could account for the movements. But there are two ways by which he *could* have induced the motion. The first would be by blowing, while the second would be by slightly kicking the table with his legs. It was therefore unfortunate that the physicist's legs could not be seen in the film, but were hidden under the table.

Dr Krmessky's work certainly cannot be ignored. But based on the few reports which have found their way to the West, it is impossible to make any decisive judgement about his claims. Luckily, though, the Soviet Union and its satellite nations are not the only countries that can boast of potential PK subjects. They have shown up in the United States as well.

Stable-system PK crosses the Atlantic

Films showing Kulagina at work have been shown over the world, and in 1971 one of them was shown at the Maimonides Medical Center in Brooklyn, New York. It had been obtained by the hospital's chief administrator, who had recently returned from a leave of absence during which he visited the Soviet Union. The audience for the showing consisted mostly of the staff and volunteer helpers at the hospital's dream laboratory, which at the time was also one of the finest parapsychology labs in the country. In the audience that day was a haematologist named Felicia Parise, who had previously been one of the lab's best ESP subjects. Miss Parise was peculiarly affected by Kulagina's performance. She could not wait to get home and try to imitate her; since she simply knew she could do the same thing. Felicia kept up her enthusiasm for several months. Each day when she got home from work she would take out her trusty plastic vial and concentrate on moving it, but nothing happened.

These months were trying ones for Felicia, since her grandmother, to whom she was deeply attached, was dying at the hospital. The obsession with developing PK became her means of psychological escape. '. . . I could hardly wait each night to get home for a quiet period with my plastic bottle', she later admitted. 'That was the only time I could stop thinking about the heartbreak and tragedy that was coming on at the time. It became such an obsession that I took my plastic bottle to work and tried to move it during lunch hours and coffee breaks.'

This ritual went on for several months, but when Felicia finally did move the bottle it was under very different circumstances. She had come home from work one evening and was taking off her artificial eyelashes. She was about to put them away for the night, in a little alcohol bottle in the kitchen, when the phone rang. It was her mother, who hurriedly told Felicia that her grandmother had taken a turn for the worse. Felicia tried to compose herself and prepared to rush back to the hospital. She ran to the kitchen to grab her eyelashes when the little bottle slid away from her hand as she reached for it.

Felicia's grandmother died shortly after the incident. Felicia kept practising and several weeks later she discovered that she could now move her bottle by exercising her will — although it took a tremendous amount of effort. She at first kept her talent confidential and would not demonstrate it for anyone. During this time she also expanded her repertoire of PK effects by gradually learning to move plastic vials and deflecting a compass needle.

Charles Honorton was a senior research associate at the Maimonides lab at the time and was also a close friend of Felicia's. He became the first outsider and parapsychologist to witness her PK. As Honorton reported to the 1973 convention of the Parapsychological Association, which convened that year in Charlottesville, Virginia:

> Late in the summer of 1971, while in Durham, North Carolina, I received a letter from Parise in which she reported success in displacing a small alcohol bottle, presumably by PK. When I returned to New York I was invited to her home for a demonstration. The alcohol bottle was actually a small clear plastic medicine bottle (59 mm high and 34 mm in diameter), filled approximately one-fourth with denatured alcohol. Parise used this bottle to preserve her cosmetic eyelashes. As we arrived in the kitchen, she placed the bottle on the formica countertop, approximately one foot back from the edge of the counter. She placed her hands on the edge of the counter, then silently looked at the bottle for two to three minutes. At that point she exclaimed that the bottle had moved. I did not see any movement. Parise was silent for another minute or two. Then the bottle moved one and one-half to two inches to my right and away from her. I then picked up the bottle and examined it carefully to be sure there was no moisture present and nothing attached to it, then replaced it on the counter to see if it would slide by itself. The bottle did not move. Later, Parise again placed her fingers on the edge of the counter. This time the bottle began slowly to move forward and to my right, in a curved trajectory. It stopped and started again three times and finally (after reaching a distance of approximately four and one-half inches from its starting position) reversed direction, returning toward me, and then stopped. [42]

Honorton then spent considerable time examining the countertop to see if there was any normal way he could get the vial to slide. He failed, no matter what procedure he used. Honorton also told his colleagues that:

> During the following months I had occasion to repeat these observations, under the same conditions, a number of times. Parise became successful at deflecting the needle of a small pocket compass. In working with the compass, she would frequently place her hands, cupped slightly, à la Kulagina, around the periphery of the compass, about six inches over its surface. Often I would unexpectedly pass her hands directly over the face of the compass to insure against concealed metallic shavings, etc. In no case did similar movements occur when I did this.

In order to produce her PK, Felicia would strain violently. This might actually have been a 'learned' behaviour she picked up from watching films of Kulagina, who had first inspired her to try her hand at PK. However, the bottle first moved totally spontaneously, so we know that strain is not necessary *per se* in order for Felicia's PK to activate. This was a discovery that Honorton was also able to make one day during a social visit Felicia was making to his lab:

> PK attempts in the laboratory were always a strain for Parise, and she was not confident there. While she never succeeded in moving the bottle in the laboratory, she did succeed on a number of occasions in producing good compass deflections. On one occasion, while she was in my office, I tried to coax her to 'zap' my own compass. She was in a hurry to leave, and did not want to get 'worked up' for PK. However, I prodded her, and as she stood about 18 inches from the desk on which the compass lay, she waved her arm in the direction of the compass and jokingly said 'Abracadabra'! The compass needle immediately reflected 90 degrees.[42]

Two other investigations were made of Parise's psychokinetic abilities. The first was undertaken by Honorton himself, when he decided to film the PK at Felicia's apartment. The cameraman he brought along was an amateur magician and even he was impressed. Honorton was able to film Felicia moving her vial and deflecting a compass needle; other segments of the film show Felicia moving a piece of foil and deflecting the compass needle while both were covered by bell jars.

Further tests with Felicia Parise

After he had fully documented Felicia's claims, Honorton took her to the Institute for Parapsychology in Durham, where tests with her were designed and executed by Graham and Anita Watkins, who were both research associates at the Institute. Their tests resulted in some interesting surprises.[89]

Their first tests were conducted in a downstairs lab room. Watkins placed a bottle on the coil of a metal detector behind a glass shield. Packets of film were set around the bottle at varying distances. Felicia stood some distance away and tried to influence the set-up through the shielding, but failed — even when a compass was substituted for the bottle. She was getting disheartened, so she finally asked if the glass could be removed. The Watkinses then brought out the entire set-up, film and all, and placed it directly in front of her. The psychic concentrated, her body jerked and trembled, and the compass needle began to deflect. 'When the movement of the compass needle was finally accomplished,' Watkins reported, 'it was accompanied by a change in the sound frequency produced by the metal detector, whereupon a total shatter of the tone occurred; this could be artificially simulated only by placing a very large metal mass (a two pound roll of solder) in the field coil.'

The compass needle had deflected by about fifteen degrees and remained lodged there! The Watkinses at first thought that the compass was simply broken, but as soon as they took it away from the experimental area it returned to normal. The needle automatically deflected when it was carried back into the specific area of the room where Felicia had been displaying her PK. It took twenty-five minutes for this PK-generated 'field of influence' to dissipate. Later the Watkinses found that the film packets that had been laid around the compass were all exposed, the degree of exposure increasing in proportion to each packet's proximity to the compass.

Unfortunately, Felicia does not practise her PK anymore. She gave it up about two years after she started, for a number of reasons — including the simple fact that demonstrating the phenomenon was a total drain on her. Neither could she handle the fact that her friends and associates were eyeing her suspiciously and with scepticism. Even her close friends could not believe in her powers and Felicia could not stand the alienation that she knew she would have to face if she continued with her psychic development.

Assessing the evidence

There is more photographic documentation testifying to Nina Kulagina's powers than there is for the accomplishments of any other contemporary psychic. Several sceptics have claimed that she simply fakes her displays by the use of threads or strings. But this facile theory cannot explain how she can move objects in totally sealed chambers, or move a single match placed alongside a large mass of matches without easily being detected. Kulagina has also performed a number of feats that no simple theory of sleight-of-hand can explain — such as separating the yolk from the white of an egg, and accelerating and/or diminishing a frog's heartbeat. The collected evidence supports the conclusion that Kulagina possesses some sort of psychokinetic ability similar to that possessed by the great physical mediums of yesteryear.

Similar points could be made about the research undertaken with Felicia Parise, although the cases of Alla Vinogradova and Julius Krmessky remain too controversial and unclear to serve as evidence for the existence of PK.

6.

The Geller Effect

I doubt if Uri Geller needs an introduction. Back in the 1970s he was undoubtedly the best known and most controversial psychic currently on the parapsychological scene. Through his PK and ESP demonstrations he converted several sceptical scientists to the cause of parapsychology.

Born in Tel Aviv on December 20, 1946, Geller first noticed his psychic abilities while he was still quite young. He claims that he first learned that he was psychic when his mother gave him a watch for his seventh birthday. 'I could see the hands move ten minutes, fifteen minutes. Nobody touched the watch,' the psychic told *Time* magazine writer John Wilhelm. 'Always it happened in class. Then I knew things had to happen when people were around, because I'm using their energy.' PK was not his only childhood power, since — again by his own claim — he would often psychically guess how well his mother had done at her frequent card games.

Uri moved from Tel Aviv to Cyprus when his mother, who had been divorced, remarried. There he attended private school, learned English, and remained for several years before returning to Israel when he was nineteen. These were trying times for Israel and Uri, like most Israelis, volunteered for military service, became a paratrooper, and fought in the Six-Day War of 1967. He was wounded but recovered, and was discharged soon afterward. It was while he was recovering from his war wounds that Geller met Hannah Strang and her brother Shipi. They became close friends and Shipi has been Geller's constant companion on his tours and public appearances. This too, of course, has encouraged several sceptics to charge that he is Geller's trained accomplice.

Uri Geller (BBC Hulton Picture Library)

By 1968, Geller was free from his military obligations and was out looking for a job. His first employment hardly foreshadowed his eventual emergence as an internationally known psychic, since he worked in the orders department of a textile company. However, it was during this period that Geller began giving semi-public theatrical performances of his alleged psychic powers. Most of these earlier demonstrations consisted of feats that sound, in retrospect, more like a standard stage magician's tricks than psychic wonders. Geller would be blindfolded and then would describe or duplicate drawings scrawled on a blackboard, guess numbers written out by members of the audience, and so on. These were hardly very original stunts, but his demonstrations became rather popular events in Tel Aviv, so Geller left his job with the textile company and turned to show business.

His repertoire soon became fairly extensive. He would guess colours, numbers, or city names written on a blackboard; telekinetically repairing broken or stopped watches, and bending metal by touch came later. It was this last stunt that jolted Geller into the limelight. A man who could bend metal by the power of the mind was certain to make it big on the show business circuit, so this type of demonstration soon became Geller's speciality.

It was at this point in Geller's career that his claims came to the attention of Dr Andrija Puharich, a physician from the United States, who has long been interested in the paranormal. Dr Puharich flew to Israel to watch Geller perform and resolved to bring him back to the United States for scientific tests.

Geller became better known in the United States after meeting Puharich, who did everything in his power to bring him to public awareness. The two also astounded the public with a new claim. Geller's psychic gifts were not inborn abilities, maintained Puharich, but were gifts from the space people who were working through him! Nor did Geller's claims stop there, for both Geller and Puharich were soon asserting that they had become the *emissaries* of these space people.

Despite these extravagant personal claims, many notable scientists became interested in Geller and his apparent ability to bend metal psychically, to dematerialize and rematerialize objects, and perform other psychic feats. Although his theatrical background tended to discredit his psychic claims, several important scientists quickly became converted when they witnessed some of Geller's more startling PK effects. Some of their testimonials still remain hard to refute.

One of these incidents was reported by Gerald Feinberg, a physicist from Columbia University and one of America's most esteemed scientists. The incident occurred when Feinberg was having lunch with Geller, Puharich, ex-astronaut Edgar Mitchell, and Mitchell's secretary, one day in August 1972 at the Stanford Research Institute in Menlo Park, California. Geller suddenly decided to give one of his impromptu but impressive demonstrations, and asked Mitchell's secretary to take off her gold ring. She clenched it in her fist, while the psychic waved his hand over it. He then asked her to open her fist. As Feinberg explains:

> She opened it up and the ring then appeared with a crack in it, as if it had been cut through with a very sharp instrument. Initially there was a very small space, probably a fraction of an inch. It looked essentially like a whole ring, but with a crack going through it. But even more interesting, he took the ring and put it down on a table where several of us were sitting. Over the period of a couple of hours, the ring twisted. It had originally been a circle with a crack in it, but over the period of two or three hours it twisted so that it went gradually into the shape of an 'S'. It didn't twist fast enough that you would actually see it happen, but if you looked every fifteen or thirty minutes you could see the angle increasing.[76]

This narrative is typical of the reports which came out about Geller during these years. It is a fascinating anecdote, but one that prompts many more questions than it really answers. For example, the sceptic would want to know how everyone was seated. Did Geller touch or handle the ring after it was placed on the table? What happened during the fifteen or thirty minute periods when no one was watching the ring? Where was it placed down? Was it placed near Geller or across the table from him? Why didn't they monitor it or put a glass over it?

An even wilder — yet more impressive — anecdote was reported by former astronaut Edgar Mitchell. This incident took place during a lunch Geller and several scientists were having at the S.R.I. cafeteria. Geller was undergoing a series of tests there at the time and was lunching with Mitchell and Harold Puthoff, a physicist at S.R.I. Geller was eating his ice-cream when his spoon struck something hard. It turned out to be a broken tie-pin. Mitchell took the broken tie-pin from Geller and casually examined it. But his nonchalant attitude was soon transformed into wild enthusiasm when he recognized it as identical to one which had been presented to him three years before by a company that he was working with.

This may have been only an amazing coincidence, but the story does not end there. The three gentlemen were walking back to one of the lab rooms a few minutes later when *another* little metal object fell to the floor. The scientist picked it up and ascertained that it was the other half of the tie-pin previously discovered in Geller's ice-cream. Mitchell was impressed but, verbally addressing the alleged intelligences behind Geller's powers, made what was to be a prophetic remark. 'I wish they could bring something back we could be one hundred percent sure about,' he exclaimed. Another metallic clink was heard in response and there, on the floor between Mitchell and Puthoff, was yet another tie-pin. This one had a pearl head. Much to the surprise of his colleagues, Mitchell became tremendously excited; for he claimed that the tie-pin was identical to one which he had lost four years before! It had been a present from his brother, who had purchased it in Japan. To prove his point, the astronaut showed Geller and Puthoff that at the back of the tie-pin was an old brass navy pin. Mitchell then explained that he himself had substituted the pin for the original one years before.* [90]

Scientific tests with Uri Geller

Because of the controversial claims that Geller was making, a group of researchers interested in parapsychology decided that the Israeli psychic should undergo testing under scientific conditions. Money was procured for the project which was eventually turned over to Russell Targ and Harold Puthoff, who were carrying our parapsychological research at the Stanford Research Institute. Both Targ and Puthoff were originally laser physicists who had become enamoured with psychic studies, and were then spending much of their time studying this challenging new science. So in November 1972 Geller flew from Europe to California to participate in what was to be two series of experiments. [85]

Targ and Puthoff at first only tested Geller's PK informally, since they were more interested in focusing on his claimed ESP abilities. Their results can only be considered suggestive but by no means proof of his PK powers. They first took Geller to a special lab room and tried to determine if he could alter the readings on a magnetometer.† the psychic was searched for hidden magnets and then asked to concentrate on the device.

* When I first read about this series of incidents, I phoned Dr Puthoff at S.R.I. about this remarkable story. He assured me that Mitchell's account was accurate as far as he could recollect.

† A magnetometer is a device which measures the fluctuations in a magnetic field. It is connected to a strip chart recorder which inks out a continuous record of the fluctuations. Normally a magnetometer is insensitive to jarring, but a magnet or static discharge around it will make the pen wiggle.

Targ and Puthoff later testified that when Geller passed his hands over the device the recorder did in fact show a little 'jump'. However, they could not definitely rule out artifact or fraud as the cause of the anomalous recording.

The two researchers were, however, encouraged enough to proceed with their tests, so they next asked Geller to offset a one-gram weight balanced on an electric scale. This weight was placed under a metal can which was also balanced on the scale. The entire system was then enclosed by a bell jar. Geller was able to cause a deflection of the recording pin that registered an effect on the weight. But, unfortunately, floor vibrations or a host of other normal factors could cause similar deflections, so they could not be ruled out as possible explanations for the effect. While at S.R.I. Geller also demonstrated his metal-bending and his ability to deflect a compass needle but never under conditions which would conclusively preclude fraud.

However, the real substance of the S.R.I. work was a series of ESP experiments especially designed by Dr Puthoff and Russell Targ. Their findings prompted a debate over Geller — and the S.R.I. tests — that even today has not been resolved. For these tests, Geller was taken to a 'room-within-a-room' sort of chamber on the ground floor of one of S.R.I.'s buildings. He was placed in the chamber while the researchers — and several other people — remained just outside it. They then placed drawings on the wall of the outside room, while Geller was asked to report over an intercom what the pictures depicted. He was extremely successful at this task, sometimes describing the drawings in remarkable detail.

This experiment prompted the researchers to publish their findings on Geller's ESP in the October 1974 issue of *Nature*, one of England's most respected science journals. The editors of *Nature* were a bit reluctant to publish the report, and even prefaced it with some critical comments — especially criticizing its lack of details and chiding the researchers for not using truly random targets. They were also unhappy that more information was not presented about what safeguards against fraud had been incorporated into the tests, since it represented (in their view) a valid scientific approach to the study of the paranormal.

Nature's publication of the S.R.I. report caused a storm in traditional scientific circles. A lengthy editorial reply to the report soon appeared in *New Scientist* charging that the S.R.I. researchers had been duped by Geller. It also reported gossipy behind-the-scenes comments which pointed out rumoured weaknesses in the S.R.I. work, even claiming that Geller had actually been caught in fraud. The *New Scientist* editorial continued by accusing the S.R.I. scientists of selectively reporting only a few of their tests with Geller and of whitewashing what they called the 'circus atmosphere' and 'lax conditions' which had pervaded the tests. Probably the most serious charge levelled during the controversy between *Nature* and *New Scientist* was that Shipi Strang, Geller's long-time companion, was always present and 'constantly underfoot' during the experiments, and could have served as Geller's accomplice. The charges went on and on and nothing was really resolved, but the credibility of the S.R.I. report — in the minds of many — had suffered considerably.

It was also true that some evidence was forthcoming that Geller *had* resorted to fraud at times during his S.R.I. stay. It later came out that when several American scientists visited the S.R.I. lab in December 1972 to meet and test him informally, they felt that they had caught Geller trying to hoodwink them. [90]

The current status of this celebrated *Nature* report still remains a matter of debate. Toward the end of 1981, however, *Fate* magazine in the United States sent me to S.R.I. to look into several charges being made against the quality of this research. I was able to examine the location of the experiments, and spoke with several people who had taken part in them. My conclusion was that the tests *had* been conducted under scientific control and that many charges being levelled against them were unfounded.

The case against Uri Geller

Uri Geller thus presents an unfathomable enigma to all who have worked with him or observed his demonstrations. Is he a showman or a psychic? Or is he a mixture of both? It is hard to say. One problem that the open-minded sceptic faces involves the difficulties in evaluating Geller merely by reading written reports about him. Many of these accounts read rather impressively, but just do not give enough information for us to make a judgement about whether anything genuinely paranormal really occurred. Take a look back, for example, to the 'ring' incident that Feinberg talks about and which was quoted earlier. It certainly looks as if Geller produced genuine PK in this instance. But yet we would have to restage the entire sequence of events carefully in order to determine what access Geller might have had to the ring. The verbal account that the Columbia University physicist placed on record is too incomplete to be taken at face value. Sad to say, *most* reports on Geller's PK powers are worthless as scientific evidence. The following example will serve as a case in point.

For some years, one of Geller's most enthusiastic supporters was Dr John Taylor, a professor of mathematics at King's College in London.[87] Geller visited Dr Taylor at the college on June 20, 1974, to participate in some tests the professor had designed to see if the psychic could bend copper strips. Here is part of Taylor's report:

> Geller tried to bend the copper strip without direct contact, but had not done so after several minutes; there was no significant change in the properties of the thin wire. We broke off in order to start measuring his electrical output, but turning around a few moments later, I saw that the strip had been bent and the thin wire was broken.
>
> Almost simultaneously I noticed that a strip of brass on the other side of the laboratory had become bent. I had placed that strip there a few minutes before, making sure at that time that it was quite straight. I pointed out to Geller what had happened, only to hear a metallic crash from the far end of the laboratory, twenty feet away. There, on the floor by the far door, was the bent piece of brass. Again I turned back, whereupon there was another crash. A brass strip on the table had followed its companion to the far door. Before I knew what had happened I was struck on the back of the legs by a perspex tube in which had been sealed an iron rod. The tube had also been lying on the table. It was now lying at my feet, with the rod bent as much as the container would allow.
>
> None of the flying objects could have actually been thrown by Geller as he was some distance away from them and would not have been able to get close to them without being spotted. I was not wholly surprised because an earlier occurrence in the corridor had led me to expect something of the sort might happen. I was walking along with Geller after the first batch of tests when a strip of metal, which had been left on the desk in my office, suddenly fell at my feet. We were at least seventy feet from the office when this occurred. I have to admit Geller could have brought the thing out of the room with him.[86]

In one sense, this account is typical of the material that has been published about Geller. So let's take a look at it in detail.

Notice first that Dr Taylor admits that he never saw the wire bend; but only saw it (in his own words) upon 'turning around a few moments later'. Not only is it obvious that Taylor had his back turned at the critical moment, but it is impossible to determine just where Geller was standing during this time. Nor is the reader given any details about the number of minutes that passed between when the experiment was concluded and the discovery of the bent wire. Just how long is a 'few moments'?

The next paragraph of Dr Taylor's account is just as revealing, and is filled with similarly unanswered questions. Since Dr Taylor's attention was still riveted on the first target, his back must have been turned on the second strip. This situation could have given Geller ample time to engage in some hanky-panky. In fact, it becomes quite obvious that the PK only and always seemed to occur when the physicist's back was turned. It is therefore hard to take seriously his claim that 'none of the flying objects could have been thrown by Geller...' While many anecdotal reports about Geller's PK sound very impressive, they fall apart when critically examined. What we need are better reports about Geller's PK, and better designed tests as well. The so-called tests I have personally witnessed have *not* been impressive.

I first met Uri Geller in May 1975. Our meeting was certainly impromptu since we bumped into each other in an elevator at a New York publisher. The next time I met him was in Los Angeles on June 6. My colleague, Raymond Bayless, and I had heard that Geller was going to appear on the Lou Riggs show over radio station KCRW, a small Santa Monica station just off the campus of Santa Monica City College. We drove to the station hoping to watch the interview and got there precisely at four o'clock which was the time that Geller was also scheduled to arrive. Geller was late as usual and didn't arrive until four-forty. His tardiness was in one respect opportune, for it gave Raymond and me time to do a little leg work around the station.

First we interviewed the stage hands, who were very excited about Geller's appearance. They were all believers and were eager to see his metal bending and telepathic feats at first hand. So it was immediately plain to us that Geller could be assured of a sympathetic audience. One employee had even brought along a watch which he claimed had not run for five years. He told me that if Geller could get it running it would prove that his abilities were genuine, as far as he was concerned. I asked to examine the watch, and the employee had no qualms about allowing me to handle it. I found, much to my amusement, that I could get it running for several seconds merely by quickly jabbing the back of the case. I pointed this out to the man, but he said nothing and just put the watch back into his pocket.

When Geller finally arrived with Shipi Strang, he made a more than regal entrance. Preceded by his entourage and greeted by an admiring crowd of enthusiasts, Geller looked like the crown prince of some European nation. Geller recognized me, greeted me cordially, but then disappeared into a back room to confer about the programme and to give one or two little demonstrations. I stayed in the control room so that I could secure for myself a good vantage point from which to watch the interview.

Geller came back into the studio a few minutes later and sat down at a small table opposite his host. I remained in the control room watching everything through a window, while Raymond stayed in the booth with Uri. He then left and went into another adjoining room where he could watch the interview through a window, but from a different perspective to mine. Shipi Strang was present as well, but on Geller's instructions stationed himself away from the interview chamber and well out of the psychic's view.

The interview then began. After talking with Riggs for a few minutes over the air, and answering some questions, Geller dipped into his repertoire of demonstrations, which I was able to watch very carefully. He began with some rather unimpressive ESP tasks. He first covered his eyes and told the interviewer to make a simple drawing. But I could see from my vantage point that Geller was peeking through his fingers, so he had little difficulty reproducing what Riggs had drawn.

Geller then announced that he could set broken watches in motion and, sure enough, he was immediately approached by the same technician whose watch I had started only an hour before. Geller tapped the watch forcibly as Riggs continued the interview, and at one point toyed with the winder. He aborted the interview a few moments later to announce enthusiastically that the watch was ticking. But to my own mind Geller had done nothing to the watch that I had not done earlier. The technician, nonetheless, then announced over the air that the watch had not run at all in the last five years. This was blatant nonsense, as I well knew.

It was during all the commotion over the watch ticking that the next 'phenomenon' took place. Someone in the booth suddenly cried out that the watch hands had jumped several minutes ahead of where they had been set previously. Another victory for Uri? Hardly. Remember that I had seen him toy with the watch while he was being interviewed, so he had ample opportunity to reset the hands. I also noted that when Geller handed the watch back to Riggs, he fumbled and dropped it onto the wooden table between them. This might have been accidental, but such a jab will tend to get many run-down watches ticking for a few seconds or longer.

Geller's only other feat during this series of demonstrations was his metal bending, which was the one thing I had most wanted to see personally. Several small metal objects were laid before him, including a few keys which had been collected earlier that afternoon from those of us observing the interview. I focused my eyes directly on any item

Geller was handling, for I wanted to make sure that he did not fraudulently bend any of them before going on to another item. (I was guessing that he would probably bend an object surreptitiously and then go back to it later, rehandle it, and then pretend that it had bent paranormally at that time.) I tried to keep my eyes from wandering from the objects Geller was playing with, concentrating on not becoming distracted by any superfluous motions he might make with his other hand. Geller toyed with several objects on the table before finally deciding to bend a key. The key was lying flat on the table and I could see that it was not yet bent. From that point onward, my eyes never left the key at any moment. Raymond, too, kept his eyes glued on it. Here is his written account as to what happened next, which corresponds to my own observations:

Mr Geller placed his hands over a key for some minutes but never held his hands in a position which would gain him normal leverage. Frequently he held it between two fingers and periodically stroked it with one finger. He infrequently transferred the key from one hand to the other to 'stroke' it but during this transfer no vigorous muscular pressure was seen. The position in which the key was held would only allow very little muscular force to have been used. I watched intently to see if any muscular effort would show and such was not the case.

I saw that the key was bent about 8° as it was held 'edge on' to my view. The key was a heavy, standard 'front door' specimen and after the interview had ended I examined it and attempted to bend it but could not. Probably, if I had exerted all my strength I could have bent it, but such an effort would have been ridiculously obvious. Further, I would have had to use both hands in such an effort. The key belonged to a member of the station's staff and when I questioned him he identified it as his house key.

At the beginning of the bending of the key I continually watched for the opportunity to 'sight' along it and was able to do so more than once. The key was perfectly straight. Further, the key never left Mr Geller's hands and there was no possibility for a substitution to have taken place; I watched for this possibility in particular.

Geller had kept the key in open view at all times, and at no time did he 'duck' it under the table or to the side of his chair in order to bend it fraudulently. Substitution could not account for the bend, nor could Geller have previously bent it. If the key had been fraudulently bent, Geller could only have done it through manual force. I cannot dismiss this possibility, although neither Raymond nor I saw him grip the key in any way which would allow him the leverage to bend it. On the other hand, people do not realize how strong human fingers can be, and I have seen keys and nails bent by a single hand in a most impressive manner by fraudulent 'psychic' metal-benders.

I must admit that I was rather impressed by Geller's demonstration, but my attitude changed later that day. When the interview was over, Geller suggested that Raymond Bayless and I — whom he now knew to be parapsychologists — go into a back room at the station to show us some special effects. No one followed us into a back conference room, so it was just the three of us. He suggested various ESP tests that he would like to try and we let him go ahead, although I was able to see exactly how he was faking each and every one of them. The tricks were not even very original, although they were marvellously well-executed.

The case for Uri Geller

Even though it seems quite obvious that Uri Geller is part charlatan, I see no reason why he could not also possess genuine psi capabilities. Fraud does not necessarily exclude the genuine, it merely complicates it. Although Geller has been caught in fraud, there are still several experiments and anecdotal reports on his PK that cannot be easily dismissed. No consideration of Uri Geller would be fair or complete without examining some of these accounts in some detail.

One of the most noteworthy investigations into Geller's PK was made by W. E. Cox, who was then a research associate at the Institute for Parapsychology in Durham, North Carolina. Cox visited Geller at the psychic's New York apartment on April 24, 1974, and during the meeting was able to carry out two especially intriguing PK tests.[18]

During the first experiment, Geller and Cox faced each other over a glass-topped coffee table. Geller suggested that they begin the session with a key-bending trial, so Cox handed him a flat and ungrooved blank key. Geller seemed a bit nonplussed and told the investigator that he preferred to work with a more personal key and enquired whether Cox could supply one. Cox stated that he only had the one key available in order to force Geller into using it. (It was two and quarter inches [16cm] in length, made of steel, and virtually unbendable by hand.) Geller examined the key and then returned it to Cox, suggesting that he place it flat down on the edge of the coffee table. Cox placed his own finger on one side of the key, while Geller began stroking the rest of it gently. Since the key was lying flat on a transparent glass table top, Cox could be sure that it had not been bent in advance of the test. Yet as Geller continued to stroke the object, it slowly began to bend upward. As Cox explains:

> The key was flat upon the glass table, touching along its length. My right forefinger pressed upon one end of the key with only a normal force, and Geller's right forefinger gently stroked the rest of the key as he stood bending over the coffee table. I took advantage of the table's transparency to gain a view of the underpart of the key with the aid of a mirror I held in my left hand. Light from a window, at 6:15 p.m. EDT, enabled a relatively clear view. The top of the key, of course, could be seen directly, with Geller's finger touching it. After making several strokes, he said it was bending, then raised his hand and pressed his end of the key so as to rock it approximately one-eighth of an inch. He slid the key from under my finger and again rocked it, expressing some pleasure. I resumed control of my end of the key, bringing the mirror into use at this point. Geller then resumed stroking the key until it bent to an angle of about 12¼ degrees. The entire event, I would judge, took less than a minute.
>
> The temperature of the part of the key under my finger did not appear to change. What is more important is that the position of my end of the key did not change, except when Geller first rocked the key. The distance between my eyes and the key throughout the test was no more than one and a half feet. Intentionally, I had exerted no strong pressure on the key, nor did the normal downward pressure of my finger vary more than it might have if Geller had met with complete failure.

A specially prepared Hamilton pocket watch played the key role in Cox's second and more novel test of Geller's powers. Since many people claim that Geller has been able to start their broken clocks and watches, Cox decided to rig a watch so that it could not possibly run. In that way, a critic could not argue that the watch had merely been jarred or knocked into running. It is relatively easy to get an old watch started again momentarily by any number of means; but Cox was 'one up' on Geller. He had placed a piece of aluminium foil inside the watchworks, thereby obstructing the balance wheel. This successfully prevented the watch from operating at all. The foil had been placed on the balance wheel and beneath the regulator arm in such a way that even vigorous shaking could not dislodge it or get the watch running. Geller, of course, was totally ignorant as to the way the watch had been prepared. He merely took the time piece, shook it, and held it to his ear. Despite all of Cox's precautions, the watch started ticking after Geller had shaken it and worked with it for about a minute. Cox later opened the watch and discovered that the foil, which had been very securely placed in position, had been mysteriously moved. Nonetheless, there seemed no normal way that Geller could have manipulated the foil manually or fraudulently.

While Cox's tests are impressive, an even more startling experiment was carried out with the psychic in October 1973 (and later again in 1974) by Eldon Byrd, a scientist with the Naval Surface Weapons Center in Silver Springs, Maryland. Byrd's first test was carried out at the centre itself, while the replication was done at a private home in Connecticut.[10]

When Byrd first met Geller in October 1973 he brought along two pieces of nitinol wire, a rather curious alloy that was at the time not generally available commercially. Now nitinol's most peculiar property is that it retains a 'memory' of the shape in which it was manufactured. So no matter how it is bent, creased, or crumpled, it will always return to its original shape after heat is applied to it. Lighting a match under it is enough to do the trick. Byrd of course wanted to see whether the Israeli psychic could permanently deform the wire, so he cut it into three lengths and then handed one to Geller:

> Geller asked me to hold the wire. I held it tautly between the thumbs and index fingers of both hands, keeping it very straight. Geller put his thumb and index finger over the wire and started to rub back and forth. After about twenty seconds of rubbing the wire Geller said he felt a lump forming in the wire. When he removed his fingers, the wire had a definite 'kink' in it . . .

But what happened next really astounded Byrd:

> I asked that some boiling water be brought in. This particular wire was formed, at the time of manufacture, in a straight configuration, and immersion in boiling water should have caused it to spring back vigorously to that shape. *But when I placed it in water, the wire, instead of snapping back with some force into a straight shape, began to form approximately a right angle.* I lit a match and held it over the kink, but still the wire did not straighten out . . .

Byrd later had the wire X-rayed, but the examination revealed nothing. An X-ray crystollographic analysis was then made which uncovered a slight alteration in the structure of the kinked section of wire.

After these results became known, several metallurgists at the Naval Surface Weapons Center where Byrd worked became fascinated by the 'paranormally' kinked wire. They even put it under tension in a vacuum chamber and heated it almost to the point of melting. But when the wire cooled, the kink re-formed as stubbornly as ever. Byrd could find no way to straighten it out; the wire is apparently still on exhibition somewhere.*

The 'Geller effect'

Both the Cox and Byrd experiments seem to have been conducted under conditions that eliminated fraud. But since it appears as though Geller is not above sleight-of-hand tricks on occasion, these experimental reports cannot stand alone as proof of Geller's alleged powers. However, a few cases of spontaneous PK have also occurred in Geller's presence under conditions that make' fraud unlikely. Even taking into account mal-observation, errors of memory, and Geller's ability to manipulate his observers, some of these reports seem unshakable. They, too, deserve to be considered by anyone trying to evaluate the phenomenon of psychic metal bending. One of these impressive reports was placed on record in June, 1975, by Arthur Zorka, a magician and member of the Occult Investigations Committee of the Society of American Magicians, Atlanta Chapter. Mr Zorka was present at the filming of a television performance given by Geller that summer, and later that day Geller gave the magician and some of his colleagues a private demonstration. According to Zorka:

> The first test involved Uri Geller's attempt to bend a fork that I provided. The fork was made of forged steel, with a nylon-reinforced handle. I specifically selected this fork because of its extreme resistance to physical stress. I placed the fork in Mr Geller's outstretched hand. His fingers curled around it, and in moment, without the fork's leaving my sight for even an instant, it literally exploded, sending fragments across the room.[63]

Since Zorka has published photographs of the fragments, we have a valuable record of this little experiment. These photographs were published by Charles Panati in his anthology, *The Geller Papers*. From the pictures it is clear that the metal part of the fork was not distorted. Only the nylon-reinforced handle was actually broken. This makes me wonder whether Geller could have broken it with a hand or, having first distracted his investigators, with an implement. This seems rather unlikely. In a letter he wrote some time later to a fellow magician, however,

* The only criticism of this experiment I have come across was made by Martin Gardner in the April/May issue of *The Humanist*. Gardner points out that on occasion he himself has been able to kink nitinol wire permanently, and that the wire *was* available to magicians at the time of Byrd's experiments.

Mr Zorka admitted that, 'The sound that came from Geller's hand after he clenched his fingers around the handle was not unlike the sound ice makes as it cracks in warm water.' Now this is just the sound that would have been produced had Geller crushed the handle with his hand. So Zorka's report is impressive, but not proof of Geller's PK.

On the other hand, a more convincing instance of metal bending has been reported by Dr Thomas P. Coohill, a physics professor at Western Kentucky University. The actual incident took place at Dr Coohill's own home during a social get-together with the psychic:

> We did not ask Geller to bend anything for us at lunch, nor did he suggest that he do so. However, after we had eaten Geller and I went into the living room and began talking about caving . . . After about a minute we both heard a metallic 'clink', it sounded as though something metallic was dropped on a solid floor. Looking around, I saw a spoon behind my desk. It was bent . . . [16]

This initial part of Dr Coohill's testimony is not very impressive. It is quite conceivable that Geller could have distracted the physicist and thrown the spoon quickly. But as Dr Coohill continues:

> As I held it in my hand and called the other people into the room, the spoon suddenly began to bend in another place (at right angles to the handle . . .) It seemed as if the spoon were observed by all present . . . The incident further amazed me since the floor to my living room is thickly carpeted. Where the 'clink' came from I cannot imagine.

Personally, I am not over-impressed by the 'clinking' sound Coohill describes. The noise could have easily been caused had Geller thrown the spoon against the desk behind which it fell. Since the room was thickly carpeted, the spoon would not have made any noise as it fell to the ground after striking the desk. The result would have been a sudden metallic noise and nothing more; but it is, nevertheless, hard to dismiss Coohill's claim that the fork bent right in his own hand and in full view of several independent observers. It seems to me that Coohill is either deliberately lying, which is not likely, or something very remarkable happened that afternoon.

Yet a third example of a spontaneous 'Geller effect' has been reported by Danish magician Leo Leslie in his book, *Uri Geller*.[50] Leslie had been initially sceptical of Geller's claims, but had the opportunity to meet the psychic in January 1974 when Geller was scheduled to appear on a Danish television programme. Leslie had been called in to 'coach' the television personnel on how to spot trickery, if Geller should resort to it. The most surprising upshot of the show, however, was that Leslie himself became one of Geller's most enthusiastic converts! During the course of the show, Leslie watched as Geller performed his usual programme of ESP and PK effects. He was impressed but still sceptical, and told Geller so when the two met after the programme was over. Geller always likes a challenge, so he asked the magician to test him personally and under his own conditions. Leslie was delighted, but not prepared for the metal bending feat that Geller had in store for him:

> After his demonstration of telepathy Geller tried psychokinesis. A nickel-plated, enamelled key was given Geller. He asked the journalist who was present to hold the key between two fingers. Geller then rubbed it a couple of times, very lightly, with his forefinger. 'I can't do it,' he suddenly said. 'You have done something to this key. I cannot get in contact with the metal.' I immediately suspected that Geller probably uses a chemical to soften metal, and that with the coating on the key he felt defeated. I took the key from the journalist and studied it closely. But while I sat looking at the key the enamel suddenly started to crack, and a second later strips of the nickel plating curled up like small banana peels, while the key actually started to bend in my hand. I don't know who was more excited, Geller or the rest of us in the room. I only know we were all thrilled.

Leslie's encounter with Geller is the most impressive in the growing literature on his feats. It is clear in this instance that the metal was seen to bend while Leslie held the key. Many witnesses claim that Geller has bent metal in their own hands, but rarely have any of them actually seen it in the process of deforming.

Could these metal bending feats be due to fraud? If the metal really bent when Geller was not touching it, fraud seems highly unlikely. By far, though, the most commonly voiced explanation for this type of bending is that Geller uses a corrosive chemical to soften the metal that he plans to bend. This theory, however, cannot explain many of his metal bending accomplishments. While it is true that you can soften metal by soaking it in a solution of metal halide, this causes the metal to become brittle. It will simply snap if pressure is put on it, and will not actually bend. This is very different from the type of effect that Geller likes to demonstrate. Several other chemicals can be used to weaken metal such as diluted nitrate of mercury or aqua regia. But these are highly corrosive materials and it is inconceivable that Geller would be able to manipulate these chemicals while being watched in a brightly lit room.

Assessing the evidence

In the light of reports such as these, I think it is highly possible that Geller can bend metal psychokinetically. How often he does it, I don't know, since it is equally certain that he will bend metal fraudulently if he thinks he can get away with it. This is the puzzle that makes Geller the mystery man he has become. How much genuine PK does Geller possess? How often does he cheat? I don't think anyone could give reliable odds on that one!

7.

PK by Committee

In the summer of 1972 several members of the Toronto Society for Psychical Research embarked on a rather unique experiment. They decided to see if they could conjure up a ghost! The upshot of their experiment was fascinating. The Canadian group discovered that, by hard and long practice, they could generate a collective 'group' PK force, even though none of them, individually, seemed endowed with any special psychic ability. [61]

The Philip experiments
If you saw a ghost, how would you react? Would it appear real to you? Or perhaps it would look misty and unreal. Would you realize that it was an hallucination or would you mistake it for a living person? The Canadian group certainly took up a formidable challenge when they decided to tackle the subject of ghosts, since phantoms are perhaps the most enigmatic form of psychic phenomena.

They realized that, to study ghosts best, they would have to be able to produce one on demand. The group proceeded by sitting week after week — meditating together, concentrating together, and forming a mutual emotional bond. By using this strategy they hoped that they could produce a collective 'thought-form', i.e. a ghost manufactured by their own minds.

The leader of the project was Iris Owen, the wife of well-known parapsychologist, A. R. G. Owen; the rest of the group consisted of other Toronto residents whose professions ranged from accounting to engineering. None of the group laid claim to any special psychic abilities. In order to make sure that the 'ghost' they conjured up really was a projection from their own minds they decided to create a wholly fictitious character upon which to focus, and named him 'Philip'.

To help focus on the Philip personality, one member of the group wrote out a fictional biography for him. The group decided that he had been an aristocratic Catholic nobleman who lived in seventeenth century England. Frustrated by his beautiful but frigid wife Dorothea, he had taken a mistress named Margo. Eventually Dorothea discovered her husband's affair, denounced Margo as a witch and husband-stealer, and had her burned at the stake. Philip, who had not defended Margo at her trial because of his dangerous political position, threw himself from the castle battlements in remorse soon afterward. One of the group members even drew a sketch of Philip as he was supposed to have appeared in life.

The group meditated together week after week. They studied Philip's life and loves and attempted to make him come to life in their minds. The procedures they used for the experiments were simple. They would sit around in a circle and mentally conjure Philip forth in the hope that eventually some sort of apparitional form would materialize in the circle. Often they would discuss Philip and his life among themselves, filling out and elaborating on the original story. In reminiscences about these sessions four years later, Mrs Owen admitted that, 'Not only had Philip himself become more 'real' to them, but . . . the story had become so familiar to them that the group members were beginning to find it more difficult to believe that Philip had never existed.'

Eventually these meditation sessions began to pay off. Sometimes one or two members would feel some sort of intangible presence in the seance room, or would receive a vivid mental picture of Philip. But, needless to say, no apparition ever actually materialized.

The group decided to change its strategy after months of generally fruitless sittings. Since the meditation practices had not worked too well, they thought that perhaps a different way of going about the experiments might fare better. By this time, Mrs Owen had chanced upon some research reports written by K. J. Batcheldor, a British investigator who had succeeded in witnessing strong PK effects by the use of sitter groups similar to her own. He achieved these results by seating a group of people around a table with their hands placed on it. He would then get them to joke and laugh until the table started to move under their fingers and even levitate. These levitations were adequate proof that no one was merely pushing the table. What was so fascinating about Batcheldor's work was that the British psychologist had (and has) never worked with a gifted medium, but feels that strong psychic energy can be generated by a group working co-operatively.[4]

After reading Batcheldor's reports, Mrs Owen changed battle plans. They followed Batcheldor's suggestions by sitting around a table and making quite a social occasion of the experiments. Gone was the gloom and austerity that had typified their meditation sessions, and they began achieving results almost immediately. For according to Mrs Owen:

> One evening, during the third or fourth new session, the group felt a vibrating within the table top, somewhat like a knock or rap. It is correct to say 'felt' rather than 'heard', because the group was making a degree of noise at the moment so that the unexpected action within the table took them completely by surprise. They were not expecting anything of that nature, so nobody could say for sure whether they *heard* the vibration as a noise, although everybody *felt* the vibration.[61]

This was only the beginning. More and more knocks resounded from the table as the sittings progressed, and finally it began to slide under their fingers. When one of the sitters openly queried if 'Philip' was the agency responsible for the movements, a rap resounded from the table top as though in answer.

The group adopted a code — one rap for yes, two for no — by which they could communicate with the intelligence behind the table motions and raps. Of course, this personality immediately claimed to be none other than their imaginary seventeenth-century nobleman.

The group learned more and more about Philip and this strange new PK force they were liberating as they evolved psychically. Often the raps would freely answer questions asked by the sitters, but would only answer in accordance with the basic story that the group had manufactured. If he were asked a question about his life upon which the group had never figured out an answer, the table would only emit annoying sawing sounds. Raps would also greet people entering the room, and as the Toronto group continued sitting, the table motions also became more spectacular. It would sway to and fro, raise up on one leg, bounce about, and so forth, then raps would answer questions put to it by the group. Sometimes these 'conversations' would become rather lively as Philip began developing a distinct personality. If the group asked Philip about his life and loves he might answer in any number of ways. The table would rap 'no' loudly if a question were asked which Philip felt to be too private. On the other hand, forceful and enthusiastic raps would issue when he was asked about his love for Margo. These raps, which sounded like wooden thuds, would come directly from the table top.

Assessing the Philip phenomena

The first question with which we have to contend when analysing the Philip work is an obvious one: can fraud account for the phenomena that the group experienced? This certainly seemed *a priori* possible. While I am not making any sort of specific accusation to this effect, neither do the early records of the Philip circle impress me as offering very good evidence against it.

To start off, we must take a look at the table movements that the circle began achieving. It seems almost impossible to rule out subconscious or even conscious pushing as an explanation for them. Remember that the circle consisted of eight members. If any one of them started pushing the table, undoubtedly the others would follow suit automatically and unconsciously. (I have seen this happen many times during my own investigations of various table-tilting groups.) Soon you will get an avalanche effect and the table will be cavorting about, but certainly not paranormally!

Mrs Owen was herself apparently very aware of this problem and tried to counter it in her book on the Philip experiments. She argues that, 'a strict watch was kept on the sitters to make sure that there was neither involuntary rapping or obvious pushing when the table was in motion.' But how could such a watch be kept when everyone was busy working with the table? In order to control better against fraud, at one point the Toronto group placed paper doilies on the table and under their hands during the sittings. The table still continued to shift about, completely unaffected by the safeguard. But does this prove the genuineness of the table movements? Not really, for paper doilies will not necessarily impede fraudulent actions. There is, in fact, practically nothing you can put on a table which will prevent fraud one hundred per cent effectively. The only thing I know of that does work is liquid facial cleanser; spread evenly over the table top, the liquid will keep the sitters from gaining traction. Unfortunately, no tests using this substance were ever attempted.

By the time I personally met some of the Philip circle, they were no longer sitting together. I was, however, able to view a film of one of their sessions, which was released by George Ritter Films Ltd. of Canada, in 1974. It presents part of a table turning session, while another segment shows the group receiving allegedly paranormal raps. The film was very similar to other private ones I had seen, and the table movements are not very exciting. The table can be seen jiggling about, rearing up off two legs, and carrying out other manoeuvres. But I have seen these same effects produced fraudulently dozens of times. Now the documentary claims that some of the table movements depicted in the film could not be imitated fraudulently; so after viewing the documentary, my colleague, Raymond Bayless, and I propped up a table at my home to find out. We were able to imitate all of the motions we had been shown — and even the more unusual ones — with total ease!

Now I do not wish to imply that the Philip phenomena are nonsense. I am being critical in order to emphasize a point: the table motions recorded by the Philip group during the early phases of their development do not, in themselves, stand up as very good evidence for PK. But what about the raps?

The raps are harder to explain away, although there are many ways to produce them fraudulently. As the Philip experiments proceeded, however, the psychokinesis became more complex, and gradually the sitters encountered types of PK effects which still remain extremely difficult to explain away. The group was eventually able to produce raps on the walls of the seance room as well as on the table; sometimes these were produced at the direct request of the sitters. Even the table movements became more interesting. Mrs Owen later recalled that:

During the January 1974 sessions there were again different movements of the table. On at least two occasions, *one* leg only was raised from the floor, causing some distortion of the table top, as the other three legs were still firmly on the ground. On each of these occasions much force was needed to push the table top down and the raised leg back into place. It felt as if the table was resisting the persons pushing down, and on one of these occasions four people were needed to push the leg down again. Once, when the table had flipped over, as described earlier, the group sat down with their hands on the exposed underside of the table and carried on a conversation with Philip. The raps became audible from the top side, which was lying flush with the carpet.

During this session an experiment was made with the candies which Philip was supposed to like. Usually candies were placed around the table for each member of the group, always with one set aside for Philip. Someone jokingly made a move to take 'Philip's' candy, telling him to hang on to it. The table was at that moment tipped at an angle of 45 degrees, and the candy stayed on the table. Two or three different types of candy were tried, and care was taken to see that they were not sticky. All of them stayed put. Subsequently the table was tipped manually, and the same candies placed on the table. They slid off almost as soon as the table was tipped, and much before the 45 degree angle achieved by Philip in action. [61]

These phenomena should be considered evidential. Very similar effects were noted by investigators who conducted seances with D. D. Home, the Fox sisters, and others back in the nineteenth century. These researchers, too, noted how the seance table would prop up on two legs and remain rigid, resisting any attempt by the sitters to push it back down to the floor. Tables would swing about during these old-time seances, yet objects placed on top would remain stationary as though glued tightly in place. Needless to say, fraud cannot easily account for these types of phenomena. The Philip circle was even able momentarily to levitate the table completely on two occasions.

Unfortunately, the Philip group eventually became bored with the sessions and by 1977 had all but ceased sitting together. They felt that they did not need to go on, having proved their point about producing a 'fictitious' communicator purely by their collective will. The Victorians, who were imbued by Spiritualist teachings and practices, usually thought that table-tilting placed them in contact with discarnate intelligences. The Philip circle dramatically demonstrated that small groups of people, by sitting together, can develop formidable psychokinetic powers — even if no specific member lays claim to psychic ability. Mrs Owen humorously calls this phenomenon 'PK by Committee'. These discoveries shed quite a bit of light on tales of paranormal table-tilting and associated phenomena in general.

Paranormal table-tilting and levitation: historical research

Table turning is a much maligned subject, and I am afraid that few scientists take it seriously. Ever since the close of the nineteenth century parapsychologists have ignored table-tilting, since so much of it can be due to subconscious muscular movements and pushing. But while most table turning is no doubt due to this cause, the literature on the subject is scattered with accounts that are difficult to dismiss lightly.[56]

One of the first scientists to study table turning in any depth was Dr Robert Hare, a chemistry professor emeritus from the University of Pennsylvania. He carried out his work during the middle of the nineteenth century. To test the movements of the table, he mounted a plate on top of it; between the plate and the table top were placed several little balls which acted as rollers. By using this set-up, the plate would roll on the balls (while the table itself would remain stationary) should the subjects or medium shove the table manually. However, Hare found that some of his subjects could move the table even when his fool-proof guard covered its top. Similar findings were made in England when table-tilting

Robert Hare constructed this device to determine 'whether the manifestations attributed to spirits can be made without mortal aid'. In his 1855 report he offered evidence that they could. (Mary Evans Picture Library)

became all the rage a few years later. For example, Sir William Barrett — who was later to help found the S.P.R. — chanced upon a table-tilting group in 1876 whose feats he felt could not be explained away normally. The following is an extract from his account:

Mr and Mrs C. willingly allowed me to make a personal investigation, and I went to their home the next day after breakfast. It was ten o'clock in the morning, and the sun was shining. Mr C., Mrs C., Florrie, and I sat around a large dining table without a cloth. The French windows which gave on to the lawn let in floods of light, so that the hands and feet of those present were seen perfectly. We soon heard a sort of rubbing, then blows on the table and on the backs of our chairs. The hands and feet of Florrie were closely watched: they were perfectly still at the time when the noises were heard. It was as if someone were hammering small nails into the floor, and my first thought was that there were carpenters on the floor above or in the room underneath, but we made sure that there was no one there. The blows became louder when we began a cheerful song, or when there was music; they then beat time in a most amusing way and changed into a rhythmical scratching, as if a violin bow were being rubbed on a piece of wood. I placed my ear many times on the exact place from which these sounds seemed to come, and I perceived distinctly the rhythmical vibration of the table without discovering any tangible or visible cause above or below.[2]

Barrett at first thought that Florrie was the principal cause of the raps but soon found that the table movements could occur even in her absence. As his report continues:

. . . One day, in broad daylight, her parents and I were sitting at the big mahogany table in the dining-room. Twelve persons could easily have been seated at it. Our hands were on the table, well in sight, when suddenly three feet of the table were lifted sufficiently high for me to pass mine under the castors. Anyone who tried to do it with all his force would find that even by grasping the table, which none of us did, it could not be accomplished without much difficulty, even by a clever and vigorous man.

On another occasion we heard raps after we had withdrawn our hands and had moved away from the table. While the hands and feet of all were perfectly visible, *and nobody touched the table,* it started moving sideways unequally. It was a heavy four-legged table about four feet square. At my request the two feet nearest to me rose up, then the other two, eight or ten inches above the ground, and the table remained there for several seconds, while nobody touched it. I moved back my chair and it advanced toward me (nobody touching it) and finally got right in front of my chair, so that I could not leave it. When it was under my nose it rose up several times, and I could convince myself by touch and sight that it did not rest on the ground, and that no human being could be directing its movements. Sceptics are at liberty to suppose that the table was moved by invisible threads worked by an imaginary accomplice who would have had to float in the air without being seen. That was my first experience of physical phenomena. Taken with later ones and other testimony they left no doubt in my mind. There is a hidden intelligence behind these manifestations. This is an extraordinary affirmation, which destroys all the foundations of materialism.

Investigations by de Gasparin and Thury
The most detailed, systematic, and eye-opening studies of paranormal table turning were not carried out in England, however, but in Switzerland in the 1850s by two innovative researchers. Both the Count Agénor de Gasparin and Professor Marc Thury spent months experimenting with table turning and both apparently witnessed some phenomenal PK. But,

interestingly enough, each of them came to different conclusions about the nature of the PK on the basis of their independent studies.

De Gasparin carried out his investigations between September and December of 1853.[27] Only a year later he published detailed records of his experiments in a massive book entitled *Des Tables tournantes du Surnaturel en général, et des Ésprits*. From these records one can see that his work was conducted under strict control. De Gasparin experimented in full light with a thirty-two inch (80cm) diameter oak table which rested on a three-footed column. The table turning team consisted of between ten and twelve people and met at his home. But instead of simply placing their hands on the table uncontrolled, de Gasparin made his sitters place their hands palms down with fingers outstretched. The thumb and little finger on each hand had to touch its neighbour's on either side, and the sitters had to maintain that position throughout the session. De Gasparin hoped that this procedure would help control conscious or unconscious pushing. Despite this control, the team found that they could usually get the table moving after only about five minutes.

Even at the onset of his experiments, de Gasparin realized that the PK force which manipulated the table was extremely powerful. During one of their first sittings, a 190 pound (90kg) man even sat on the table, yet it completely levitated from the floor, shoving him off in the process. The Swiss investigator noted how the group members would become unusually exhausted after a particularly active session and he also gradually became one of the first psychical researchers to appreciate the role that the psychology of the individual sitter plays in the production of PK. 'When a person is in a state of nervous tension, he or she becomes positively unfit to act upon the table,' he wrote. 'It must be handled cheerfully, lightly, deftly, with confidence and authority, but without passion.'

Notice how similar this prescribed setting is to the one that the Toronto group employed. They, too, were not able to generate PK until they began experimenting in a light-hearted sociable setting. De Gasparin also discovered that certain individuals completely *inhibited* movements of the table.

He made many discoveries about the PK process itself. For instance, he observed that the table motions seemed sympathetically linked to the physical movements of the sitters. As he recorded of one session:

Seeing that everything was going according to our wish, and having decided to try the impossible, we next undertake an experiment which marks our

A table-turning seance at the Swiss home of the indefatigable de Gasparin, circa 1853. (Mary Evans Picture Library)

entrance into a wholly new phase of the study and places our former experimental demonstrations under the guarantee of a positive irrefutable demonstration. We are going to leave probability behind and dwell with evidence. We are going to make the table move *without touching it.*

At the moment when the table was whirling with a powerful and irresistable rotation, at a given signal we all lifted our fingers, and continuing to form the chain a little above the table, we continued our circular movement. To our great surprise the table did the same; it made in this way three or four turns! We could scarcely believe our good fortune; the by-standers (witnesses) could not keep from clapping their hands . . .[27]

De Gasparin went on to say in the report that on two occasions the table momentarily stopped swirling when the sitters had raised their hands a little too high above it. The table resumed its revolutions when they lowered them. As they proceeded with these experiments, de Gasparin and his friends were ultimately able to produce several levitations; yet neither thermometers nor compasses held near the table registered any peculiar readings.

However, de Gasparin was more than merely interested in just witnessing PK table movements, he also wanted to discover the basic nature of the force itself and explore the nature of the intelligence that guided it. His many discoveries led him to believe that the table movements were produced by a 'psychic fluid' housed in the body. The innovative researcher also tended to reject the popular notion of his day that table turning was caused by discarnate intelligence. He believed instead that the PK was produced solely by the sitters, and could be triggered by an act of will.

Professor Marc Thury, following up on several leads uncovered by de Gasparin, published his own researches into table turning in 1855. His massive volume, *Les Tables tournantes considerés au point de vue de la question de physique générale qui s'y rattache,* presented a critical examination of de Gasparin's experiments, highlighted by observations and evaluations drawn from his own personal experiences. Thury was a professor of natural history and astronomy in Geneva, so his primary interest was in discovering the physical principles underlying table turning. But in one sense he was even more cautious than his predecessor. Before actually experimenting with his own group, he figured out a way to monitor the table mechanically in order to make sure that no one could push it without being detected. Even with these controls, he witnessed the same type of motions that de Gasparin had written about in his book.

Professor Thury's theories about table-tilting echoed his predecessor's in some respects. He, too, suspected that the table turning force which generated the movements emanated from the sitters and was manipulated by their will, but he rejected his colleague's notion that PK could only be projected by a *conscious* act of will. Thury's views were based, in part, on studies he made with a family in Geneva who were accomplished table-tilters. Sometimes they would lose control of the PK, which would break out spontaneously in their presence. Dr Thury gives this account of one of these impromptu displays:

A week had scarcely rolled by . . . when a child of the family, he who had formerly succeeded best in the table experiments, became the actor, or the instrument, in strange phenomena. The boy was receiving a piano-lesson, when a low noise sounded in the instrument and it was shaken and displaced in such a way that pupil and teacher closed it in haste and left the room. On the next day, M. N. who had been informed of what had happened, was present at the lesson, given at the same time — namely, when the dusk was coming on. At the end of five or ten minutes he heard a noise in the piano difficult to define, but which was certainly the kind of sound one would expect no musical instrument to produce. There was something about it musical and metallic. Soon after, the two front legs of the piano (which weighed over six hundred and sixty pounds) were lifted up a little from the floor. M. N. went to one end of the instrument and tried to lift it. At one time it had its original weight which was more than the strength of M. N. could manage; at another, it seemed as if it had no longer any weight at all, and opposed not the least resistance to his efforts. Since the interior noises were becoming more and more violent, the lesson was brought to a close, for fear the instrument might suffer some damage. The lesson was changed to the morning and given in another room situated on the ground floor. The same phenomenon took place, and the piano, which was lighter than the one up-stairs, was lifted up much more; that is to say, to a height of several inches. M. N. and a young man nineteen years old tried leaning with all their might on the corners of the piano, which were rising. Then one of two things happened: either their resistance was in vain, and the piano continued to rise, or else the music-stool on which the child sat moved rapidly back as if pushed or jerked.[27]

Thury noted humorously that, 'I do not think that anyone will be tempted to attribute to the direct muscular effort of a child eleven years old the lifting up of a weight of 440 pounds.'

So, long before psychic research became a psychological science, Thury had already discovered that psychokinesis was basically an unconsciously directed force. Basing his views on his Geneva investigations, the Swiss professor argued that the unconscious mind also had a will and can use it to direct and manipulate PK even without the aid or even knowledge of the conscious mind. He contended that at the psychic level there is really no difference at all between 'unconscious desires' and conscious will. He left open, however, the idea that sometimes spirits of the dead could communicate through the table movements.

The research of W. J. Crawford

Organized psychical research showed no serious interest in the phenomena of table-tilting and levitation until news of a new exciting case was reported from Ireland in 1914. In that year, Dr W. J. Crawford of Queen's College, Belfast, began what was to be a six year research project with the Goligher family, who had been practising group table levitation sessions for some time. [20-22] Mr Goligher's eighteen-year-old daughter, Kathleen, was the primary source of the psychokinesis, but all the family members seemed to be jointly instrumental in producing it as well.

The Golighers were a very ordinary family, who also happened to be Spiritualists. The sitters included Mr Goligher, his four daughters, a son, and a son-in-law. They would sit around a table in dim but reasonable light, and sing and play music until the table began to move, levitate, make sawing sounds, or emit raps. The Golighers felt that these rather varied phenomena were caused by spirits of the dead, and they communicated with these intelligences through raps similar to the way that the Toronto group talked with Philip. The family came to the attention of Dr Crawford in 1914, who soon undertook a series of tests with them for the purpose of studying the mechanical aspects of the psychokinesis. These studies lasted for six years, up until the time of his death.

Dr Crawford realized quite early in his investigations that young Kathleen was the focal point of the group's collective PK. He attended several initial seances and, by placing her on a scale, learned that her weight increased proportionately every time the table levitated. There also seemed to be a psychic bond between the medium's body and the levitated object, for the table would fall back to the floor if Crawford passed his hand between it and the medium.

By studying several of these levitations, Crawford developed a novel theory about the PK. He believed that the force behind the Golighers' PK acted like a cantilever. He calculated that the force travelled in the form of a beam from Kathleen's body to the floor beneath the object,

Investigator William Crawford obtained permission from the spirits before taking this photograph of Belfast medium Kate Goligher raising a table with the help of ectoplasm. (Mary Evans/Psychic News)

anchored itself, and then projected upwards raising the object along with it. He felt this theory could explain many aspects of the Goligher phenomena, including the fact that objects placed on top of the levitated table did not increase the medium's total weight. It also explained why a full-grown man could sit on top of the table without causing it to fall. On other occasions, however, Dr Crawford thought that the PK projected directly from Kathleen's body, proceeded directly under the table, and then lifted it up. He considered that this process could explain why on a few occasions the young woman's body would fall forward from her chair if heavy weights were placed on the levitating table.

Crawford also believed that these PK levers could account for raps, which often caused Kathleen's body to jerk concordantly. Her body was, in fact, drastically affected by the seances. She usually lost considerable weight during the course of a sitting, sometimes as much as fifty pounds (20kg)! But most of this weight would be returned to the body by the end of the session. Crawford also made one curious observation about Kathleen's powers, which I have never seen noted with any other medium. If she touched any object in the act of levitating it would immediately fall back to the ground.

Even though the Golighers sat as a family team, it certainly looks as if the PK was produced solely by Kathleen. So why has this work been included here under the heading of group PK? The answer is simple for, as his research continued, Crawford eventually discovered that somehow *all* the sitters — including himself — contributed to the power. By checking all the sitters' weights before and after the experiment, he found time after time that everyone attending a sitting lost a little weight, usually from two to six ounces (50-200g). This indicated to him that either everyone was contributing a small amount of substance or energy to the PK, or that Kathleen was somehow drawing power from the group.

The history of the Goligher circle became somewhat controversial after 1920. Crawford had a nervous breakdown that year and committed suicide shortly after. From what I have been able to ascertain by examining some private archives on the matter, he killed himself during a momentary recovery when he realized that his mental lapse might become permanent. So we can probably accept his own statement that his suicide was in no way related to his Goligher experiments. (Critics of his work have suggested that he killed himself when he discovered that the Golighers were defrauding him.)

The Society for Psychical Research had been encouraged by Crawford's report, and they sent Fournier d'Albe to investigate the circle and make an independent report. Unfortunately, d'Albe had a primarily negative reaction to his meetings with the Golighers, and was constantly annoyed by their singing during the seances. So in his report to the S.P.R. he argued that the singing was merely a manoeuvre that the Golighers used to cover up noise they were making while they faked the levitations. Even the S.P.R. officials — who had no great belief in physical phenomena even by this time — realized that the report was ridiculous and declined to publish it.

It might also be noted that, shortly before his death, Crawford successfully photographed the psychic cantilevers whose existence he had postulated.[22] These pictures — which admittedly look rather suspicious — were included in his last book on his research, *The Psychic Structures at the Goligher Circle*. They represent yet another mystery about the Goligher circle.

Assessing the evidence

Group PK phenomena, or 'PK by Committee', just may be the most important aspect of psychic phenomena that we should be exploring. The history of parapsychology has been preoccupied with the desire to locate and test gifted subjects who could levitate tables with the raising of a hand or move objects with the twinkling of an eye. But is this really necessary? It may not be. Table turning practices and home circles seem to be an obvious way of developing fairly strong psychokinesis without the need for a gifted medium. In fact, a group may be able to produce PK more consistently than a psychic can. If so, a home circle group might provide a valuable laboratory for the parapsychologist. The fact that many groups have been able to achieve splendid results in good light should encourage researchers to explore this area further.

8.

Psychokinesis and Healing

Psychic healing can be defined as a psychokinetic effect on organic tissue or matter, which aids in its recovery from illness or biological damage. If PK can move an object or upset a quantum process, it seems logical to assume that it might be capable of rearranging cells and tissues or speeding up the body's own regenerative abilities. Parapsychologists learned long ago that PK can exert a considerable influence over living or organic matter. It merely took a few simple experiments to prove this aspect of psychokinesis.

PK on biological systems

Nigel Richmond carried out a novel experiment in England in 1953, which was actually elegantly simple.[75] He merely placed a drop of pond water under a microscope and watched the paramecia (which live in the water) dart about. He then divided the water drop into four segments and began 'willing' a single and temporarily immobile paramecium to travel into a certain specified quadrant. Of course, he randomly selected the target quarter for each trial and each attempt lasted fifteen seconds. The British investigator made 1,495 trials and was remarkably successful. It would seem that, by his will, Richmond had influenced the biological behaviour of a single-celled animal.

An even more provocative biologically-oriented test was conducted in Bordeaux, France, by Jean Barry, M.D., in 1968 in collaboration with the staff of the Institute of Agronomy.[3] Dr Barry decided against working with animal life and focused his attention on fungus cultures. Petri dishes containing the cultures were prepared at the Institute the day before the experiment and then placed in an incubator where they could thrive. The next day, each volunteer subject would be given ten dishes filled with the multiplying cultures. The subjects would concentrate on five of the dishes for about fifteen minutes, during which time they tried to impede the growth of the cultures. The other dishes were left as controls. Eleven subjects participated in the study and a total of thirty-nine trials were made. By measuring and comparing the growth of the target cultures to the controls, Barry was able to determine that the human mind can successfully inhibit the growth of the fungus population. Such a finding certainly gives credence to the notion that the human mind also possesses a healing force.

Experimental analogues to 'psychic' healing

Probably the best controlled, most systematic and original research into the phenomenon of healing was carried out in the 1960s by Dr Bernard Grad, an expert in experimental morphology at McGill University in Canada. Most of Grad's work was designed with the gifts of a single healer in mind. [33] Oskar Estebany is a retired Hungarian military officer who claims that he can heal through the ancient art of the laying-on-of-hands.

Dr Grad's most celebrated experiment with Estabany was based upon the healer's ability to treat mice fed on a diet deficient in iodine. This deficiency causes goitres to form, and all the mice used in the study had duly developed them. The rodents were divided into three groups consisting of an experimental group on which Estebany would work and two control groups. While treating the goitre-afflicted mice, Estebany only held the cages in which they were housed (eight to ten animals per cage) but was never allowed to gentle the animals directly. The sessions lasted only fifteen minutes and five treatments were performed a week. After twenty days a lab worker interested in healing them 'took over' the job from Estebany and continued the treatments for another four weeks. The control groups were, of course, treated quite differently. The first was left completely alone, while the other mice were given heat treatments.

The overall results of the experiment were consistent with Estebany's claims. The healer was able to retard the growth of the goitres afflicting the target mice. To make sure of his findings Dr Grad immediately replicated his research and obtained the same results. But he had not finished with the Hungarian healer.

For their next project together, Dr Grad decided to see whether Estebany could heal wounds surgically inflicted on laboratory mice. This sounds more gruesome than it really was, since the 'wounds' were made merely by removing patches of skin from the animals. Pieces of transparent plastic were then placed over the wounds and their boundaries were traced with a grease pencil. Estebany once again just held the cages of the target mice, while several of the other rodents served as the controls. Needless to say, the mice treated by Estebany healed quicker than the controls. This experiment, too, was replicated successfully.

For his next large scale project, Grad decided to focus attention on plants instead of animals in order to see just how far Estebany's abilities could reach. The researcher chose barley seeds as the target, since they germinate and sprout easily. The seeds were planted in several plots, which were then watered with a one per cent sodium chloride solution to inhibit their growth. (Tap water was substituted later on in the experiment.) Some of the beakers holding the saline solution were, however, psychically treated by Estebany, who was allowed to hold and concentrate on them. Sure enough, the plots watered with the treated solution gave a richer yield of plants than did those fed with the straight solutions.

These preliminary plant studies were designed primarily as pilot experiments for an even more enterprising project and conceptual replication. Dr Grad employed the same experimental design as in the barley tests, but this time used the services of three subjects. One of them was the same lab worker who had participated in the original goitre experiments, while the other two participants were mental patients. One of them was a depressive neurotic and the other suffered from psychotic depression. Grad, who was working from the assumption that healing might be affected by mood, expected the depressed patients to inhibit rather than stimulate the plant growth.

The results were pretty much as Grad had expected. The seeds treated with the water held by the lab assistant grew the most successfully, while those assigned to the psychotic patient grew the worst of the lot. In fact, they grew considerably worse than control plants that had been watered with untreated solution. On the other hand the neurotic's plants grew slightly better than the controls which baffled Dr Grad until he realized that the woman's mood had been radically affected by the experiment. It had improved upon learning about the nature of the experiment, and she actually became excited about it! Could it be, Grad thought, that this had caused the patient to exert a beneficial healing effect on the solution she was holding? This seems possible, although Dr Grad never explored the possibility further.

Further tests with Oskar Estebany

While Dr Grad's work suggests that psychokinesis can be used to heal, his research tells us rather little about the nature of this potentially beneficial process. Discovering clues about the nature of healing PK was left to Sister Justa Smith, a biochemist at Rosary Hill College in New York. Sister Justa was exploring the nature of the enzyme trypsin when she learned about Dr Grad's work in Canada, and soon directed her interest toward the realms of psychic healing. It struck her that psychic healing might result when a healer somehow speeds up enzyme activity in the patient's body, since such a process would help the body recover from organic damage. So she set about to prove her theory.[83]

Procuring the services of Oskar Estebany, Sister Justa instructed the healer to treat a flask containing the enzymes by concentrating on it for seventy-five minutes. Three other bottles acted as the controls. One bottle was given no treatment at all, while the other two were treated by a magnetic field (which accelerates enzyme activity) and with ultraviolet radiation (which decreases enzyme activity) respectively. Sister Justa was later able to determine that the activity rate of the enzymes in the treated flask was similar to the activity rate of those enzymes treated with the magnetic field, a finding completely consistent with her theory. Unfortunately, though, the experiment failed when she tried to replicate it.

Recent research on psychic healing

Psychic healing is a subject that never fails to arouse both public and professional interest. In a field complicated by controversy and results that cannot always be replicated, research on psychic healing is one of the few areas of parapsychological concern that promises to have a practical application in our daily lives. The fact that more and more people are seeking out alternative medical programmes has only increased the popularity of psychic healing in the United States. Perhaps for this reason, a number of projects have been recently completed on the healing dimension of the PK force.

The most thorough and critical investigation into the nature of psychic healing was reported in 1976, by a team of researchers headed by Roger MacDonald at the Washington Research Center in San Francisco. The Center is a privately endowed laboratory that devotes a good amount of its time to parapsychological research. It is also one of the best equipped labs available for such research.

Before beginning their experiments, MacDonald and his co-workers surveyed the published results of all earlier projects attempting to document the existence of psychic healing. Their plan was to replicate critically each of these earlier studies to see if they could isolate a stable effect. This earlier research (of which only a sample has been given above) indicated that gifted healers can: affect electrical and magnetic fields; produce anomalous Kirlian photographic effects; cause perturbations within a sealed cloud chamber; affect the crystallization process of copper salt; rebond water molecules; affect the growth rates of plants; inhibit the growth of bacteria; and affect the blood-pressure of hypertensive animals. This was quite an array of findings, and the San Francisco team decided to determine if they could document them. To ensure their chances for significant results, some of the best American healers were brought to the lab to take part in the project. These included the Rev John Scudder of Homewood, Illinois, Dean Kraft, from New York, and the late Olga Worrall of Baltimore, who was probably the best known healer in the United States.

Despite the formidable reputations of these healers, most of the experiments conducted in San Francisco failed. The only interesting results occurred within the plant growth tests.[51]

This critical experiment was run at the lab and followed the design originally employed by Dr Grad in Canada. MacDonald planted several dormant rye grass seeds in a series of pots. These were then separated into control and experimental groups. Beakers of water were prepared by another researcher who then asked the healers to imbue some of them with their healing energy, a process which usually took about twenty minutes. The experimental pots were watered with the treated solution while the control plants received water from those beakers left untouched by the healers. After this initial watering, all the seeds were soaked with purified water up and through the time they sprouted. The researchers hoped that the pots given the treated water would show a higher yield of plants, while they also expected the treated plants to grow taller than the controls.

It was Olga Worrall who succeeded best. The plants nourished with water that she had treated grew some twenty-five per cent taller than the control grass. Neither of the other healers produced noticeable results, however.

One of the most curious results of the project came, however, during those experiments designed to see if a healer could lower the blood-pressure of a hypertensive rat. Dean Kraft was used for one of these experiments and a rat, especially bred with high blood-pressure, was brought to the lab where it was placed in a restraint cage. The rodent's blood-pressure was recorded by a probe attached to its tail.

Kraft was only admitted into the room after the rat was prepared for the test. But an unexpected development soon clouded the experiment at this point. Despite his reputation as a gentle and humane healer, Kraft took an instant dislike to the rat as soon as he set eyes on it. He courageously attempted to heal it, nonetheless, by sending it healing energy despite his revulsion. Everyone left the room immediately after he had finished the healing. The surprise of the day came moments later when a technician re-entered the room to run a final blood-pressure reading and found that the rat had dropped dead! No normal explanation could be found for the death.

Despite the fact that the New York healer did not succeed at all in healing the rat, he is one of the few healers whose abilities *have* been scientifically studied and documented. One of Kraft's most spectacular abilities is his talent for killing cancer cells grown in special culture flasks. This phenomenon was aptly documented in July 1977 when he travelled to San Antonio, Texas, to visit the Science Unlimited Research Foundation, a privately funded lab devoted in part to parapsychological research, founded in 1972.[45] Dr John Kmetz, a physiologist by training, was the researcher in charge of the project.

Dr Kmetz chose an especially virulent form of cancer cell, the HeLa cell, for the experiments. These cells are grown in flasks and vigorously adhere to the bottom. Not even a powerful shaking will dislodge them. The cells will only detach when they die, whereupon they float freely in the solution that fills the greater part of the container. Dr Kmetz wanted to see if Kraft could increase the number of dead cells in the solution merely by focusing his healing powers on the culture. The number of dead cells floating in the solution can be determined instrumentally by a haemacyclometer, so objective results could be made quickly by running counts before and after Kraft focused on the cultures.

A total of six experiments with the HeLa cultures were eventually undertaken over a three-day period and were all run in the same way. Kmetz took Kraft and one of his lab assistants into a special room where the cultures were kept. Three flasks were used for each test. Kraft was instructed to treat one flask by holding it in his hands and focusing on it. The lab assistant, who claimed no psychic abilities whatsoever, also 'treated' one of the flasks by holding it and mimicking whatever Kraft did with his. The last vessel was left untouched as a control. A count was made of the free-floating dead cells both before and after each trial.

In his discussion on these experiments in his autobiographical book, *Portrait of a Healer,* Kraft explains that he intuitively knew during his very first trial that he would be successful at the task. 'Concentrating on the picture I'd formed in my mind of the cells,' he writes, 'I directed my thoughts to the flask and visualized a disturbance in the cell fields and the cells blowing up . . . After about twenty minutes I knew that I'd affected the cells. I sensed a definite interaction, almost a magnetic pull, between my hands and the flask.'[46]

Kraft's impression was correct. A count of the free floating cells made after the trial showed a 300 per cent increase of dead cells over the pre-trial measure. There were no significant changes in the number of dead cells in either control flask or the one held by the lab assistant. Dr Kmetz was also impressed when he looked at some of the dead cells under a microscope. It looked as though the cells had exploded internally. The young healer succeeded in obtaining the same level of success two more times during the six experiments and confirmations, although he had to withdraw from further testing when he fell ill. But more trials and confirmations were hardly needed. Kmetz was so impressed by the results that he officially reported them to his colleagues in the October 3, 1977 issue of the *Hospital Tribune.*

Nor was this the end of Dr Kmetz's research into the wonders of psychic healing. He was later able to replicate this experiment using cervical cancer cells. The healer for this later, and as yet unpublished, experiment was Matthew Manning, the well-known British psychic and healer. He, too, was able to kill the cells without any direct contact with them.

The fact that healers can possibly treat and cure cancer has also been documented by the Nutrition Institute of America in New York by way of their research with a very unlikely yet gifted healer. These exciting experiments were supervised by Gary Null, who heads the Institute, in collaboration with several colleagues.[57]

The experiments were designed as part of a major investigation into psychic healing which Gary Null has been co-ordinating and undertaking for several years now. Null is not only the director of the Nutrition Institute of America, but also Science Director for the New York-based Institute of Applied Biology which also collaborated on certain phases of the project. Null and his co-workers have travelled all over the world meeting and interviewing healers, checking on their successes and failures, documenting case histories, and collecting a small library of material on the subject. They were very disappointed in the results of their travels for they felt they had found little hard evidence documenting the unequivocal existence of psychic healing. All too often they found themselves wondering whether psychic healers really cure their patients, or whether the patients might not be curing themselves through their own will-power. They realized that the only way they could resolve the issue was through a series of laboratory experiments . . . and by using subjects who were hardly likely to contribute to their own cure. The laboratory experiments that ensued were a direct result of this field work.

The idea was to use animal subjects, and the experiment that the Institute researchers ultimately came up with was both simple and direct. They wanted to see if a healer could prolong the life spans of mice which had been inoculated with cancer cells. During their pilot tests over fifty healers were tested, but only one, a rabbi from New York, succeeded at the task and was asked back for further testing.

Rabbi Abraham Weisman is both a rabbi and cantor, and presently administers to a congregation in metropolitan New York. Weisman discovered his healing abilities while consulting a well-known healer about a minor complaint he was suffering. When the healer laid her hands on him, he felt a powerful surge of energy. 'She informed me that I possessed certain energies and asked if I would be interested in developing them,' he told Null during an interview. Jewish law does not prohibit the practice of spiritual healing, so Weisman studied the art of laying-on-hands and absent healing with two prominent New York healers. From this beginning he has partially developed his own techniques. His present method consists of moving his hands over the patient's body without touching it. Rabbi Weisman is currently a practising healer, although he takes a critical and even sceptical approach to his work. 'Although I've had some success with healing people,' he candidly admits, 'I must also add that my patients had been receiving medication simultaneously with my treatment.'

The critical phase of the Institute's experiments with Weisman was begun on July 14, 1977 and ended three weeks later. One-year-old white female mice were used. They were housed at the Institute in large plastic cages and marked for identification. Ten of the mice were injected with Ehrlich adenocarcinoma ascites fluid, which causes fatal tumours to develop. Ten other mice were injected with cancer cells but were left untreated and served as the controls. Weisman was asked to send healing energy to each of the cancerous mice and healing sessions were held each day, well through the time the mice had developed tumours. The rabbi never actually touched the mice, but treated them by holding his hands above their cages for brief periods.

The results of this carefully conducted test confirmed that Weisman possesses some sort of power unknown to conventional science. The control mice (i.e., those left untreated) lived an average of 8.9 days before dying from the cancer. Yet those mice that had been treated by the healer lived for an average of 12.8 days — some 43.8 per cent longer. When the test was replicated, using smaller amounts of cancer cells in the initial injection, the average life span for the untreated mice was 12.9 more days. The mice that Weisman had tried to heal lived on for an average of 14.9 days. What amazed the researchers was that some of the treated mice survived up to eighteen or nineteen days despite their cancers.

The evidence for long-distance PK healing

The experiments conducted at the Washington Research Center, the Science Unlimited Research Foundation, and the Nutrition Institute of America, have shown that healers can exert some sort of influence by touching or coming into close proximity with the organisms they are treating. But what about 'absent' healing — those PK-mediated healing effects which manifest even when a great distance separates the healer from the patient? Absent healing is practised today by faith healers of all types — whether they be Spiritualist, Fundamentalist, Christian Science, or Science of Mind healers or practitioners. But until recently there was little hard evidence that such a phenomenon really exists. This has all changed now, thanks to the innovative piece of research designed by Robert Miller of the Holmes Center for Research in Holistic Healing in Los Angeles, California.[55]

Dr Miller sought to determine if a healer could influence a patient even if he or she lived miles away and, most importantly, *didn't even know that a healing was being attempted*. The project was initiated in 1976 but was not completed until 1979 and has only recently been reported to the scientific and medical communities. Dr Miller recruited a total of eight healers for the experiment; four of them were Science of Mind practitioners, one was a Presbyterian minister, another was a Church of Christ minister, and two were psychic healers. The most notable of the group was Olga Worrall.

The healers were asked to treat a series of patients suffering from high blood-pressure. Several physicians known to the project co-ordinator selected the patients, who were all unknown to the healers. Those practitioners participating in the experiment were only given the initials, ages, general health problems, and the locations of the patients. A typical healer was expected to treat six patients from all over the country. A total of ninety-six patients were eventually used for the experiment, of whom only forty-eight were actually treated by absent healing. The rest were left as controls.

No patient knew whether or not he or she was actually selected for a healing, nor were the doctors advised. The physicians just had to keep track of whether their patients showed any alterations in diastolic blood-pressure, systolic blood-pressure, heartbeat rates, or general weight. These readings were continually filed with Miller. The healers were allowed to treat the patients mentally in any way they chose. Most of them, however, used similar techniques by relaxing, attuning to some 'higher power', visualizing or affirming the patient in a state of perfect health, and then thanking the 'higher power' for its help in the healing.

The experiment was successful despite the rigorous double-blind conditions under which it was conducted. Several of the patients showed a more pronounced improvement in their systolic blood-pressure than the controls. None of the other readings, however, showed any significant changes. Four of the healers were particularly good at treating the absent patients. While close to seventy-five per cent of the control subjects improved with conventional treatment, a little over ninety-two per cent of those who received the absent healing from these four practitioners showed an improvement. This is not a statistically significant result, but does show a trend in the data.

Robert Miller's own conclusions on the basis of his study are mixed. While he is satisfied that the experiment has indeed documented the existence of remote or 'absent' healing, he has remained puzzled over the unsystematic nature of his results.

Assessing the evidence
The studies outlined in this chapter are fairly representative of the status of current research on psychic healing in general. This research has presented a mixed bag of significant success mixed with inexplicable failure. There seems sufficient evidence that many psychic healers possess some force akin to PK, but the results of the experiments prompt more questions than they answer. Why, for instance, could Dean Kraft kill cancer cells in Texas but not inhibit bacteria growth in San Francisco? Why was Rabbi Weisman able to inhibit the fatal effects of tumours

while forty-nine other healers failed? And why did Miller's healers succeed in influencing the systolic blood-pressure of hypertensive patients, but not their diastolic blood-pressure?

These may seem like insignificant questions to ask when so many researchers have made such strides in scientifically documenting the existence of a healing force latent in man. But if science and medicine ever wish to harness this energy, they are first going to have to understand it. That is where the problem remains today. While it certainly looks as though a psychokinetic healing force lies within our reach, we still know virtually nothing about it nor how to stabilize it.

9.

The Case For
Mind Over Matter

How good is the case for PK? This is the natural question with which to conclude this brief survey.

Throughout the course of this book, the more spectacular expressions of mind over matter have been constantly emphasized. The violent displays of the poltergeist have been juxtaposed with the mysteries of the seance room. The promise held out by the potentials of psychic healing have been presented with the feats of Uri Geller and Nina Kulagina. These data tend to give credence to the legendary, though sometimes well-witnessed, powers of the saints and the primitive shamans — who astonished their communities with their powers or gifts of levitation, fire immunity, and psychokinetic weather control.

Parapsychology today is, however, an experimental science and not merely an observational one. The existence of psychokinesis has therefore also been a matter of experimental concern. The *real* case for psychokinesis accordingly rests upon this laboratory evidence — and upon the evidence that you and I, and not just the great psychics of the past and present, can exhibit PK under the right conditions. Considerable data have been collected that PK — like ESP — is a potential that we all possess and can develop; and considerable contemporary experimental research has helped to tempt this atavistic power out into the open. The results obtained from this research represent, in the final run, the most important evidence for the existence of PK. But in this case we are talking about very subtle expressions of this fantastic power.

PK and dice-rolling tests

Experimental research in psychokinesis was spearheaded at Duke University in 1934, when a young gambler visited J. B. Rhine at his laboratory and claimed that he could 'will' dice to fall on certain faces more often than chance would allow. Rhine was always a keen experimentalist so he quickly rounded up some dice and the two were soon huddled together in a corner of the room rolling them. We don't know the exact results of this rather informal experiment, but we do know that Rhine was apparently impressed enough to begin active PK experimentation.[71]

Soon everyone at Duke got hooked on the dice-rolling craze. Cups were used to throw them; a rectangular rotating cage was invented to flip the dice from one end to the other; the dice were thrown down baffle boards and so on. Several lengthy studies were made of the PK effect solely on dice rolling.

The real case for PK, however, came not so much from the results of these tests, but by way of a curious pattern that started cropping up in the data. By the early 1940s, Rhine had still not published any of his many experiments on psychokinetically-influenced dice-throwing. But at that time, Betty Humphrey, a bright young helper at the lab working under the direction of Rhine, made a significant discovery when she started examining all their past results. The data recorded from the Duke dice-rolling research had been recorded on score sheets that were uniformly divided into several columns. Each column was divided into twenty-four segments, one each for each die (or dice) throw for a series of twenty-four trials. There might be, for example, ten columns per sheet constituting the results for one entire experiment. Miss Humphrey found that by dividing the score sheet into four equal quarters and comparing the scores, the first quarter of the experiment consistently yielded significantly more successful dice rollings than the last quarter. If a subject had been rolling dice for 3s, for example, he might have ten successes in the first quarter, eight in the second, three in the third, and none in the fourth.

Miss Humphrey was intrigued by her discovery; she began re-evaluating the results of several other PK tests in the Duke files and found that this same pattern kept cropping up. This decline or quarter distribution (QD) effect had been occurring systematically right under the noses of the Duke workers, but only now had it been uncovered.[72] What was so curious was that Rhine had found this same pattern showing up in his ESP tests. (His subjects invariably did better at the beginning of an

ESP experiment than at any other time during the session.) This consistency encouraged him to publish formally all of his PK research, spanning nearly ten years, and announce the 'discovery' of the PK effect. The upshot was that researchers in other labs became excited about the possibility of replicating the Duke work, and several worthwhile projects were undertaken that fully confirmed the existence of psychokinesis.

Probably the most important of these replications was conducted with extreme care by Laura Dale, who was then a research assistant at the American Society for Psychical Research in New York.[24] Mrs Dale's experiment forsook the almost informal way the first Duke work was done, and she took every precaution to guard against fraud and experimenter error. She began by recruiting fifty-four New York college students to be her subjects. Each of them was tested individually to see if he or she could influence the fall of dice.

Mrs Dale began each trial by placing four dice at the top of an elevated ledge, which was connected to a plank corrugated by several baffles. A landing platform was located at the bottom of the apparatus, on which the dice would subsequently fall and come to rest after bouncing about the baffles. Each subject threw the dice ninety-six times, trying for one specific die face. Then the subject would throw ninety-six times for *another* die face until all six die sides had been used as the target. (All told, there were 31,104 die readings for the experiment.)

Mrs Dale designed her precautions wisely. Using the baffled chute ruled out any possibility that the subjects could throw the dice in specific ways to bias how they would land. (This is a old gambler's trick.) Using *all* the die faces equally as targets circumvented the argument that the dice were biased or 'loaded' through a manufacturing error.

After concluding the experiment, Mrs Dale found that the group had achieved 171 more direct hits than would be expected by chance. That may not sound like much, but such a result would only occur statistically five times in every 1000 experiments. Neither were the dice loaded, for subjects scored equally well on all six of the faces. Some interesting post-hoc findings emerged from the study as well. Further analysis of the experimental data showed that those who believed in PK seemed to do better than those who rejected the possibility. Furthermore, subjects uniformly did better on their first set of throws than at any other time during the test, which confirmed the Duke University discovery of the QD effect.

A second important confirmation of the original Duke work was published in 1955 by Dr R. A. McConnell at the University of Pittsburgh.[54] Dr McConnell primarily followed the Duke procedures but added certain refinements. He subsequently tested 393 subjects who made over 170,000 dice rolls. The raw results of this ambitious project were not, however, significant. That is, off-hand it did not look as though his subjects had been able to make the dice fall on the faces upon which they had been concentrating. But when McConnell looked at his data in greater depth, he discovered a noticeable decline effect. By comparing the pooled data taken from the first quarter of the tests with the data from the last quarter, he, too, was able to isolate a statistically significant QD effect.

Results such as these spurred the Duke researchers to go forward with their own PK research and extend it. By the late 1950s, they were designing new and more novel types of PK dice-rolling experiments. The most prominent 'new' approach to PK testing came by way of the invention of 'placement PK' tests. These experiments did not test whether PK could make dice land on a certain face, but rather tested to determine if the force could influence them to land in prescribed areas of a landing platform. The first systematic examination of placement PK was made at Duke by W. E. Cox, who ultimately became a research associate at the Institute for Parapsychology in Durham.[17]

For his first important placement tests, Cox drew a chequer-board on the bottom of a typewriter case and numbered each of the squares successively from one to six until each of them had been numbered. He then threw twenty-four dice over and over into the case while several volunteer subjects tried to will them to land on the faces that corresponded to the numbered squares. In other words, when Cox and the subjects threw for 3s, he or she tried to make more than an average number of cubes land on squares also numbered 3. And Cox's subjects were able to succeed at the task!

While following up on his placement tests, Cox went on to invent a three-tiered platform with a chute at the top where dice could be placed. When pushed off, the cubes would bounce through the chute to the first tier, then fall down a corrugated runway to a second tier, and then fall onto the bottom platform.[19] This platform was divided into several squares, each marked either A or B. So, of course, the subject tried to make those dice which were going through the tiers to the bottom land on either the A or B square more often than chance would allow.

Cox had a specific theory in mind when he designed this test. He believed that if several dice were thrown at the same time, only *some* would be significantly influenced by the subject's PK and would make it down to the landing platform. But what about the other dice? These cubes might be *negatively* affected by the force and become trapped on the upper tiers. Whatever the reason, the experiment worked. The results of 24,000 dice throws showed a strong bias for the cubes to fall on the side chosen by the experimenter.

Working independently in Sweden, Haakon Forwald was also actively investigating placement PK during the 1950s and his research confirmed the discoveries Cox was making in the United States.[70] Like his American colleague, Forwald was quite an inventor, and up until the time of his death he had over 500 patents throughout the world to his name. His attention turned to PK after he and some friends started table turning and witnessed some amazingly strong results. He found the table motions so extraordinary that he contacted J. B. Rhine, who convinced him to focus his attention on the possibilities of placement PK work. Forwald was soon experimenting at his home, using himself as the primary subject.

Forwald used a platform which led via a runway to a tabletop. Dice were placed at the top of the platform and would, when pushed, fall down the runway, bounce about, and land on the table surface. The table was divided down the centre, and Forwald would concentrate on making the cubes fall more often on the right (A) or left (B) side alternately. He discovered that he could do this successfully. He then replicated his test by using dice of different weights by fashioning them from wood, paper, steel, aluminium, etc. The composition of the dice did not seem to affect his PK performance, but he did discover an odd pattern in his statistics. Forwald found that he was successful when he threw the dice willing them first to land on the A side of the table and then, for the next trial, on the B side. But he could not get any results if he first threw for the B side and *then* for the A side. He theorized that this effect was due to his own psychological preference for the AB sequence.

For a later home experiment, Forwald once again used cubes composed of different materials. His idea was to see how *selective* the PK force could be. So for each 'throw' he used six dice, three each of two different materials while willing his PK to influence only one set of them. For instance if he used wood and steel cubes for a particular throw, he would will only the wooden ones to deflect to the target side of the table. Forwald was just as successful at this test as he had been on his previous ones. The engineer once again verified through this ingenious test that PK is not inhibited by the composition of the cubes, for his power worked equally as well on both materials.[30]

After carrying out several other successful tests, Haakon Forwald travelled to Duke University in 1957 to replicate his work in the presence of independent witnesses. While at first he did not seem able to perform well in his new surroundings, his PK eventually made a dramatic recovery and he subsequently succeeded in replicating his earlier success.

The discovery of micro-PK

Research on dice-rolling convinced most parapsychologists that PK could best be studied by seeing how it influences a moving system. It would seem that using PK to influence a system in random motion was much easier than trying to make an object move from a stationary position. This led a few researchers to theorize that the *more* random a system, the easier it would be to influence it by PK. This, in turn, prompted parapsychologists to seek extremely random systems for use as their PK targets. This search led, in turn, to the discovery of what is now called 'micro-PK' — the finding that PK can be used to influence subatomic particles and disrupt the output of high speed oscillators.

The first controlled experiment to isolate a micro-PK effect was carried out in the early 1960s by Dr John Beloff of the University of Edinburgh.[7] Dr Beloff wanted to see if his subjects could increase the rate of particles decaying and shooting out from a piece of radioactive material (as reported by a Geiger counter). This test failed but his experimental design was later successfully employed by researchers in France, where Dr Remy Chauvin and Jean-Pierre Genthon also used a Geiger counter to register substance emissions from a piece of uranium nitrate.[15] Since a Geiger counter records radiation striking it by producing 'blips' on its counter, it was easy enough for them to test their PK subjects by asking them to try increasing or decreasing the rate of emissions. They eventually tested seven subjects, all between the ages of eight and seventeen, but only two of them were successful at the task.

Research into the possibilities of micro-PK really took parapsychology by storm in the 1970s, when Dr Helmut Schmidt at the Boeing Laboratories in Seattle, Washington, started turning his attention to it.[81-2] He was one of the first physicists to devote his full-time attention to parapsychology and has probably conducted more research on PK than any other contemporary experimenter. (Dr Schmidt subsequently left the Boeing Laboratories to work in Durham with Dr Rhine. He is now in charge of a lab at the Mind Science Foundation in San Antonio, Texas.) It was Schmidt who showed parapsychologists the potential easily available to them through the use of simple equipment, which he himself started building and is continuing to invent. The most basic of these

Helmut Schmidt's random number generator seems to enable PK to be tested with the elimination of all human influence except that of the subject. (Mary Evans Picture Library)

was a machine with a built-in oscillator (coin-flipper) that speeds back and forth between two positions about one million times per second. One could say that the machine oscillates between a 'heads' or 'tails' position. Dr Schmidt hooked this machine up to a piece of radioactive strontium 90, which randomly throws off electrons when it decays. No one can predict exactly *when* an electron will shoot off, but Schmidt designed his apparatus so that the oscillator will momentarily stop when it registers an arriving particle. He hoped to find subjects who could use their psychic abilities to alter the decay rate of the particle so that the machine would be prone to 'stop' in one position significantly more often than in the other.

When it actually came to working with the device, Dr Schmidt decided to give his subjects a morale-booster, so he connected the apparatus to a panel of nine circular lights. The panel was programmed in such a way that the lights would flash more in one direction if the subject was psychokinetically influencing the decay rate of the Strontium 90. He therefore only had to tell his subjects to make the lights move in a circular pattern around the panel, and usually did not have to explain about the radioactive decay. It became a sort of 'willing' game and Schmidt found that several volunteers could succeed at the task.

Dr Schmidt's ingenious test encouraged several other parapsychologists to determine whether non-selected subjects could influence high speed oscillators, quantum processes, or noise-driven random generators. This approach to PK testing is now the predominant paradigm in parapsychology, and the micro-PK effect has been isolated and studied at several parapsychology laboratories.

PK influence on temperature

One of the more recent explorations of small-scale PK came to the forefront of interest in 1973, when Dr Gertrude Schmeidler of New York City College published her research on the effects of mind-over-temperature.[80] She began her project while testing the claims of Ingo Swann, a New York psychic who asserted that he could alter the surface temperature of an object while sitting several feet away from it. Dr Schmeidler was willing to test the psychic and set up a display of bakelite and graphite pieces connected to delicate thermistors. Swann was instructed to sit twenty-five feet (six metres) away, and asked to make specified pieces either warmer or cooler by willing it to happen. The targets were chosen randomly, and Swann was amazingly proficient at carrying out the task. There was, however, a curious outcome of the experiment that had not been predicted by Dr Schmeidler. When Swann focused on one specific piece, other pieces near it changed temperature too — but in the opposite direction! It was a sort of psychic version of 'robbing Peter to pay Paul'.

Dr Schmeidler and her associates later went on to show that the non-selected subjects also possess the ability to change the temperature readings on very delicate thermistors.

Experiments such as those that we have been discussing should serve as unequivocal evidence that PK exists. Laboratory confirmation of the PK effect concomitantly sheds added (and favourable) light on tales of rampaging poltergeists, levitating tables, and ectoplasmic materializations. For if many of us possess a small modicum of PK ability, it is logical to suppose that there may be some people who possess a storehouse of such capabilities.

But there is a more important issue which we have to address rather than simply considering whether PK exists. What is the *nature* of this mysterious force, power, or energy? Because of its almost unbelievable complexity, I don't think anyone working in parapsychology today could possibly offer a comprehensive theory that can explain how PK operates. Such a theory would not only have to account for all its different guises, from micro-PK to poltergeists, but it would also have to explain the mechanics of the process as well. Psychokinesis represents too big a mystery to be explained by any neat, trim, and facile theory. It is even possible that it really isn't an 'energy' at all, as the term is normally defined and used in conventional science.

This is an important point, for a few contemporary parapsychologists are beginning to question whether there really is such a thing as a 'psychic energy' at all. They argue that PK can be explained more easily if we simply accept the idea that mind directly affects matter and that this is an inherent principle of the structure of the Universe. We wouldn't have to worry why PK doesn't conform to the laws of physics by adopting this model, since it really wouldn't be considered a force at all. Dr Beloff believes that this might be the most fruitful approach to the study of PK. In an essay he published in 1975 he pointed out that perhaps '... under certain conditions, still to be established, an idea or intention in the mind can automatically constrain a physical system to act in such a way as to express the idea of intention. That this is, in the last resort, an ultimate fact about the world; there is no further "bridging mechanism" to be invoked to make this fact intelligible.[8]

Dr Beloff is not actually saying anything truly novel, since such a world-view would be concordant with much Eastern philosophy. Unfortunately, this theory leaves a number of questions unanswered. Why, for instance, does PK only occur under rare circumstances instead of any time we want it to? It would seem clear, therefore, that PK probably *does* represent some sort of force or energy that can be generated by human thought or will. So the real issue is to discern the basic nature of this force.

There are three likely possibilities. Psychokinesis could be: (1) a mental or psychic energy; (2) a biological plasma; or (3) a mental agency that manipulates normal or ambient energy already present in the atmosphere and then makes it act in a certain prescribed way, according to the will of the subject.

PK as a form of energy

There can be little doubt that PK does, on occasion, manifest many characteristics of an energy. It is usually invisible, causes overt effects on material objects, and so on. In other words, psychokinesis has the capacity to carry out work. This principle is especially evident when you examine poltergeist cases. Objects displaced by the poltergeist often tend to move in similar directions or follow similar trajectories in a semi-lawful manner.[77] Such findings tend to indicate that poltergeistic PK is an energy directed out from the agent which behaves according to self-regulated principles. This is how must conventional forms of energy work.

If you will recall from Chapter 6, Felicia Parise's PK also seemed to set up some sort of energy field, since a compass she had deflected continued to deflect when placed back in the area of the room where she had been displaying her PK.

PK as a biological force

Parapsychologists have also amassed considerable evidence that PK is a biological force as well as an energy. It can interact with living matter and can appear as a mist, plasma, or as a mock tissue-like structure.[32] Furthermore, psychokinesis sometimes also seems linked more to the body of the agent than to his or her mind: this is suggested by the physiological ordeals that Eusapia Palladino went through during her seances, and by the way Rudi Schneider's PK was directly linked to his respiration rate. We must also wonder how any sort of purely mental energy could be used to build up semi-physical structures such as were seen at Palladino's seances, during D. D. Home's sitttings, and created by other physical mediums of years past.

The phenomenon of materialization is a complex and controversial one, especially since the subject has been so sadly neglected by modern parapsychologists. The reason for this neglect is simple, for there just do not seem to be any mediums on the psychic scene today who are able to produce such wonders. This does not mean, however, that we have the right to reject the strong historical evidence testifying to such phenomena. [26,88]

PK as a redirective force

Some parapsychologists at present are developing a third explanatory model to account for PK. They suggest that perhaps psychokinesis is not a force at all. Instead of expending large amounts of energy to manipulate matter directly, perhaps it merely manipulates and processes normal forms and sources of energy. It might then re-order it, and then direct it to carry out our mental wishes. [79]

This idea may sound a bit confusing, but look back to Dr Gertrude Schmeidler's experiments with Ingo Swann. Each time Swann was able to make a specific thermistor (or cube) change temperature, outlying thermistors (or cubes) in the same general area altered temperature in the opposite direction. Did the PK directly affect the target thermistor, or did it actually *redirect energy from the atmosphere* which really carried out the task and which resulted in these sympathetic temperature changes? Could PK then be a 'power' that is capable of re-ordering random sources of physical or ambient energy?

This theory may seem very attractive, but it rather begs the question, since it still leaves a central issue unrevolved — i.e., what is the primary force that the psychic *uses* to re-order normal energy? There must be some mediating link between the psychic's will and this energy-manipulating process.

It should be noted that a new version of this theory has recently been proposed which suggests that PK is not a force specific to biological life at all. It may be a cosmic energy permeating all life and matter that can sometimes be *channelled through us.* Such theories are actually quite ancient and have been suggested by such disputable phenomena as so-called 'pyramid powers', Wilhelm Reich's 'orgone' energy, and even by some of the phenomena of mesmerism. [53] The existence of such a life-force remains to be proved, but the theory is at least provocative and should be considered provisionally viable.

Some personal conclusions

What then do *I* think PK is? This is a difficult question for me to answer, since it is much easier to ask questions in parapsychology than to answer any of them. The only thing that seems clear is that PK is a versatile power, and that it can re-structure itself in order to handle best each task it tries to perform. There might therefore be little connection between the process employed to levitate a table and the energy released to 'Gellerize' a key.

Frankly, I doubt if the PK process represents a consistent process at all. Please remember that psychokinesis is only a *term* we use to label and categorize a certain class of phenomena which are, as yet, inexplicable according to the known laws of science. That is all the term denotes and it is possible that different types of PK effects may be due to different processes at work. I think the evidence indicates that we may possibly control a complicated *system* of hitherto unrecognized powers and forces within our minds and bodies — including some sort of 'mind energy' which on occasion can also take on the guise of a parabiological plasma.

But these two expressions of psychokinesis could represent two independent energy systems within man. I also believe, but have little evidence to support the idea, that we might also be blessed with the ability to channel some sort of cosmic force or life-force as well. This force may be a form of primordial energy pervading the known Universe for which, on certain occasions, we might act as batteries or generators. This theory must remain only pure speculation, though.

Hopefully, new light will be shed on the mystery of psychokinesis as the study of physics and biology progresses. So, for the time being, perhaps we should not be too dismayed by our lack of understanding or even good theoretical explanatory models. Perhaps we should merely be content with studying the PK process however we can — and without any preconceptions about where our research and findings will eventually lead us.

References

1. Adamenko, Victor, 'Controlled movement of objects in bio-electrical fields', *Journal of Paraphysics*, 6 (1972): 180, 225-26.
2. Barrett, William, *On the Threshold of the Unseen* (London: Kegan Paul, 1917).
3. Barry, Jean, 'General and comparative study of the psychokinetic effect on a fungus culture', *Journal of Parapsychology*, 32 (1968): 237-43.
4. Batcheldor, K. J., 'Report on a case of table levitation and associated phenomena', *Journal of the Society for Psychical Research*, 43 (1966).
5. Bayless, Raymond, *The Enigma of the Poltergeist* (West Nyack, N.J.: Parker, 1967).
6. Bell, M., 'Francis Bacon, pioneer in parapsychology', *International Journal of Parapsychology*, 6 (1964): 199-208.
7. Beloff, John and Evans, L., 'A radioactivity test of psychokinesis', *Journal of the Society for Psychical Research*, 41 (1961): 41-46.
8. Beloff, John, 'On trying to make sense of the paranormal', *Proceedings of the Society for Psychical Research*, 56 (1976): 173-95.
9. Bender, Hans, 'Modern poltergeist research', in *New Directions in Parapsychology*, edited by John Beloff (London: Elek, 1974).
10. Byrd, Eldon, 'Uri Geller's influence on the metal alloy nitinol', in *The Geller Papers*, edited by C. Panati (Boston: Houghton Mifflin, 1976).
11. Bottazzi, Phillipe, 'The unexplored region of human biology: observations and experiments with Eusapia Palladino', *Annals of Psychical Science*, 6 (1907): 149-56, 260-90, 377-425.
12. Carrington, Hereward, *Eusapia Palladino and her Phenomena* (New York: B. W. Dodge, 1909).

13. Carrington, Hereward, *The Problems of Psychical Research* (London: Rider, 1914).

14. Carrington, Hereward, *The American Seances with Eusapia Palladino* (New York: Garrett Publications, 1954).

15. Chauvin, R, and Genthon, J., 'Fine Untersuchung Über die Moglichkeit Psychokinetscher Experiemente mit Uranium and Geigerzähler', *Zeitschrift für Parapsychologie und Grenzgebiete der Psychologie* 8 (1965): 140-47.

16. Coohill, Thomas, 'Filmed and non-filmed events: on Uri Geller's visit to Western Kentucky University', in *The Geller Papers* edited by C. Panati (Boston: Houghton Mifflin, 1976).

17. Cox, W. E., 'The effect of PK on the placement of falling objects', *Journal of Parapsychology* 15 (1954): 40-48.

18. Cox, W. E., 'Notes on some experiments with Uri Geller', *Journal of Parapsychology* 38 (1974): 408-11.

19. Cox, W. E., 'Three tier placement PK', *Journal of Parapsychology* 23 (1959): 19-29.

20. Crawford, W. J., *The Reality of Psychic Phenomena* (London: Watkins, 1916).

21. Crawford, W. J., *Experiments in Psychical Science* (London: Watkins, 1918).

22. Crawford, W. J., *The Psychic Structures at the Goligher Circle* (London, Watkins, 1921).

23. Crookes, William, *Researches in the Phenomena of Spiritualism* (London: James Burns, 1874).

24. Dale, Laura, 'The psychokinetic effect: the first A.S.P.R. experiment', *Journal of the American Society for Psychical Research* 40 (1946): 123-51.

25. Dunraven, Earl of (Lord Adare), *Experiences in Spiritualism with D. D. Home* (Reprint: London: Society for Psychical Research, 1924).

26. Eisenbud, Jule, 'The mind-matter interface', *Journal of the American Society for Psychical Research* 69 (1975): 115-26.

27. Flammarion, Camille, *Mysterious Psychic Forces* (Boston: Small, Maynard & Co., 1907).

28. Flammarion, Camille, *Death and its Mystery*, Vol. 2, *At the Moment of Death* (New York: Century, 1922).

29. Fodor, Nandor, *On the Trail of the Poltergeist* (New York: Citadel, 1958).

30. Forwald, Haakon, 'A further study of the PK placement effect', *Journal of Parapsychology* 16 (1952): 59-67.

31. Gaddis, Vincent, *Mysterious Fires and Lights* (Philadelphia: David McKay, 1967).

32. Geley, Gustave, *Clairvoyance and Materialization* (New York: Doran Co., 1927).

33. Grad, Bernard, 'The biological effects of the 'laying on of hands' on animals and plants: implications for biology'. in *Parapsychology: its relation to physics, biology, psychology and psychiatry*, edited by G. Schmeidler (Metuchen, N.J.: Scarecrow Press, 1976).

34. Herbert Benson, 'Notes on the Kulagina films', *Journal of Paraphysics* 3 (1969): 67-68.

35. Herbert, Benson, 'Kulagina cine film 'A'', *Journal of Paraphysics* 3 (1969): 89-95.

36. Herbert, Benson, 'Kulagina cine film 'B'', *Journal of Paraphysics* 4 (1970): 16-24.

37. Herbert, Benson, 'Report on Nina Kulagina', *Parapsychology Review* 3, no 6 (1972): 8-10.

38. Herbert, Benson, 'Psychokinesis in Bratislava', *Parapsychology Review* 3, no. 1 (1972): 9-12.

39. Herbert, Benson, 'Electrical PK', *Parapsychology Review* 3, no. 5 (1972): 18-19.

40. Herbert, Benson, 'Alla Vinogradova: demonstration in Moscow', *Journal of Paraphysics* 6 (1972): 191-96.

41. Herbert, Benson, 'Spring in Leningrad: Kulagina revisited', *Parapsychology Review* 4, no. 4 (1973): 5-10.

42. Honorton, Charles, 'Apparent psychokinesis on static objects by a "gifted subject"', in *Research in Parapsychology — 1973*, edited by J. Morris, et.al. (Metuchen, N.J.: Scarecrow Press, 1974).

43. Jung, C. G., *Memories, Dreams, Reflections* (New York: Random House, 1961).

44. Keil, J. H. J.; Herbert, B.: Ullman, M.; and Pratt, J. G., 'Directly observable voluntary PK effects', *Proceedings of the Society for Psychical Research* 56 (1976): 197-235.

45. Kmetz, John, Afterword to *Portrait of a Psychic Healer* by Dean Kraft (New York: Harper and Row, 1981).

46. Kraft, Dean, *Portrait of a Psychic Healer* (New York: Harper and Row, 1981).

47. Kulagin, Ing. V. V., 'Nina S. Kulagina', *Journal of Paraphysics*, special issue: *Symposium on Psychokinesis* (1971): 54-62.

48. Kulodny, Leo, 'When apples fall', *Journal of Paraphysics* 2 (1968): 105-8.

49. Laurent, Emile, 'Remarks on certain common telepathic manifestations', *Annals of Psychical Science* 5 (1907): 79-96.

50. Leslie, Leo, 'Uri Geller', exerpted in *The Geller Papers*, edited by C. Panati (Boston: Houghton Mifflin, 1976).

51. MacDonald, R. G., et.al., 'Preliminary physical measurements of psychophysical effects associated with three alleged psychic healers' (San Francisco: Washington Research Center, 1976).

52. Maigret, Pamela de, 'PK training in Russia', *Fate*, May 1976.

53. Mann, W. Edward, *Orgone, Reich and Eros* (New York: Simon & Schuster, 1973).

54. McConnell, R. A., 'Wishing with dice', *Journal of Experimental Psychology* 50 (1955): 269-75.

55. Miller, R. N., 'Study on the effectiveness of remote healing', *Medical Hypotheses* 8 (1982): 481-90.

56. Nisbet, Brian, 'Table-turning, a brief historical note', *Journal of the Society for Psychical Research* 47 (1973): 96-106.

57. Null, Gary, et.al., 'An experiment in paranormal healing', (Nutrition Institute of America, New York: n.d.)

58. Ochorowicz, Jules, 'A new mediumistic phenomenon', *Annals of Psychical Science* 5 (1909): 333-99.

59. Ostrander, S. and Schroeder, L., *Psychic Discoveries Behind the Iron Curtain* (Englewood Cliffs, N.J.: Prentice Hall, 1970).

60. Osty, Eugene, *Les Pouvoirs inconnus de l'esprit sur la matrière* (Paris: 1932).

61. Owen, Iris, with Sparrow, Margaret, *Conjuring up Philip* (New York: Harper & Row, 1976).

62. Palmer, John, 'A case of RSPK involving a ten-year-old boy: the Powhatan poltergeist', *Journal of the American Society for Psychical Research* 68 (1974): 1-33.

63. Panati, Charles, *The Geller Papers* (Boston: Houghton Mifflin, 1976).

64. Pratt, J. G., *ESP Research Today* (Metuchen, N.J.: Scarecrow Press, 1973).

65. Price, Harry, *Stella C* (London: Hurst, Blackett Ltd., 1925).

66. Price, Harry, *Rudi Schneider* (London: Methuen, 1930).

67. Price, Harry, 'An account of some further experiments with Rudi Schneider', *National Laboratory of Psychical Research* Bulletin no. 4 (1933).

68. Rejdak, Zdenek, 'Telekinesis or fraud?' *Journal of Paraphysics* 2 (1968): 68-70.

69. Rejdak, Zdenek, 'The Kulagina cine films', *Journal of Paraphysics* 3 (1969): 64-66.

70. Rhine, J. B., 'The Forwald experiments with placement PK', *Journal of Parapsychology* 15 (1951): 49-52.

71. Rhine, J. B., *The Reach of the Mind* (London: Faber and Faber, 1948 Reprint).

72. Rhine, J. B. and Humphrey, B. M., 'The PK effect: special evidence from hit patterns. 1. quarter distribution of the page.' *Journal of Parapsychology* 8 (1944): 18-60.

73. Rhine, Louisa, *Hidden Channels of the Mind* (New York: William Sloane, 1961).

74. Rhine, Louisa, *ESP in Life and Lab* (New York: Macmillan, 1967).

75. Richmond, Nigel, 'Two series of PK tests on paramecia', *Journal of the Society for Psychical Research* 36 (1956): 577-88.

76. Rogo, D. Scott, *The Poltergeist Experience* (New York: Penguin, 1979).

77. Roll, W. G., *The Poltergeist* (New York: New American Library, 1974).

78. Roll, W. G., 'Poltergeists', in *Handbook of Parapsychology* edited by Benjamin Wolman (New York: Van Nostrand, 1977).

79. Rush, Joseph, 'Physical aspects of psi phenomena', in *Parapsychology: its relation to physics, biology, psychology and psychiatry*, edited by G. Schmeidler (Metuchen, N.J.: Scarecrow Press, 1976).

80. Schmeidler, Gertrude, 'PK effects upon continuously recorded temperatures', *Journal of the American Society for Psychical Research* 67 (1973): 325-40.

81. Schmidt, Helmut, 'A PK test with electronic equipment', *Journal of Parapsychology* 34 (1970): 175-81.

82. Schmidt, Helmut, 'Mental influence on random events', *New Scientist*, June 24, 1971: 757-58.

83. Smith, Justa, 'Paranormal effect on enzyme activity through laying-on-of hands', *Human Dimensions*, Summer, 1972.

84. Solfvin, G., and Roll, W. G., 'A case of RSPK with an epileptic agent', in *Research in Parapsychology — 1975*, edited by J. Morris et.al. (Metuchen, N.J.: Scarecrow Press, 1976).

85. Targ, R., and Puthoff, H., 'A perceptual channel for information transfer over kilometer distances: historical perspective and recent research', *Proceedings of the Institute of Electrical and Electronic Engineers* 64 (1976): 329-54.

86. Taylor, John, 'A brief report on a visit by Uri Geller to King's College, London, June 20, 1974'. in *The Geller Papers*, edited by C. Panati (Boston: Houghton Mifflin, 1976).

87. Taylor, John, *Superminds* (London: Macmillan, 1975).

88. Venzano, Joseph, 'A contribution to the study of materialization', *Annals of Psychical Science* 6 (1907): 75-119.

89. Watkins, G., and Watkins, A., 'Apparent psychokinesis on static

objects by a "gifted subject": a laboratory demonstration." in *Research in Parapsychology — 1973* edited by J. Morris, et.al. (Metuchen, N.J.: Scarecrow Press, 1974).

90. Wilhelm, John, *The Search for Superman* (New York: Pocket Books, 1976).

Index

ASSAP (Association for the Scientific Study of Anomalous Phenomena) was founded in 1981 to bring together people working in different fields of anomaly research. It does not compete with other societies or organizations, but serves as a link organization enabling members of existing groups to share views and information and benefit from pooled resources. ASSAP issues its own publications, has its own research archives, library and other facilities, and holds periodic public conferences and training events in various parts of the country: ASSAP co-operates with local groups or, where none exists, may form one of its own.

ASSAP members include people from all walks of life who share a belief that it is the scientific approach which is most likely to solve these enigmas: they are neither uncritical 'believers' on the one hand, nor blinkered sceptics on the other, but are ready to go where the evidence leads them. If you sympathize with this attitude and would like to participate actively in our exciting pursuit of the truth, you may consider joining us. Write for fuller details to the Editor, c/o Aquarian Press, Denington Estate, Wellingborough, Northamptonshire, NN8 2RQ, England.